PRAISE FOR GREG REITMAN'S BOOK
ROOTED IN PEACE

"I really love this book *Rooted in Peace*. I think it is very important for today!"

—David Lynch, American filmmaker, painter, musician, actor, and photographer

The only way you can change the world is to be the change yourself. Inspirational and enlightening is Greg Reitman's book *Rooted in Peace*."

—Deepak Chopra, MD, world-renowned author and pioneer in integrative medicine

"Greg Reitman's personal journey of *Rooted in Peace* reconfirms the interconnectedness of our humanity from the inside to the outside."

—Dr. Mark Hyman, medical director at Cleveland Clinic's Center for Functional Medicine, founder of the UltraWellness Center, and *New York Times* bestselling author of *Food: What the Heck Should I Eat?*

"*Rooted in Peace* offers a profound story and fertile ground for everyone interested in growing a global culture of peace."

—J. Frederick Arment, founding director of International Cities of Peace

"From the personal to the global, a deeply uplifting and substantive book!"

—Jonathan Granoff, president of Global Security Institute

"Humanity is slowly starting to awaken to the beautiful reality that we truly are all interconnected ... *Rooted in Peace* brings this to life, creating a story rooted in our oneness with each other and Mother Nature. A much-needed book at a time of turbulence in the world."

—Jean Oelwang, president and trustee of Virgin Unite

"Greg Reitman takes us to the heart of spirit, to the core of what we must change to create a better world. This is a fine book with vivid lessons of higher consciousness for us all."

—Chris Kilham, author, educator, and founder
of Medicine Hunter

"Each time I read *Rooted in Peace,* a new layer of my life and a dream for a flourishing world opens and shimmers and then becomes whole in a new, more powerful form."

—Professor Jim (James A. F.) Stoner,
professor at Fordham University

"Greg Reitman has fashioned *Rooted in Peace* into a major statement on eco-consciousness, eco-spirituality, and eco-health. A formidable teaching tool, it is informative, inspiring, and—simply—engaging to read."

—Kurt Johnson PhD, ecologist and coauthor of
The Coming Interspiritual Age

ROOTED IN
PEACE

About the Author

Greg Reitman is an American film director, producer, executive producer, writer, author, activist, and public speaker, described by *Movie Maker Magazine* as "one of the top ten filmmakers producing content that impacts our world." He is the founder of Blue Water Entertainment, Inc., an independent production company focusing on environmentally conscious broad-based entertainment.

Widely regarded as Hollywood's "green filmmaker," Greg produced the Sundance Audience Award-winning feature documentary *FUEL*. Prior to producing *FUEL*, Greg wrote, produced, and directed the feature documentary *Hollywood's Magical Island: Catalina*. His latest feature documentary film, *ROOTED in PEACE,* won Best Feature Documentary at New York Festivals, debuted at the United Nations, and released theatrically through Landmark Theaters combined with a national DVD release in Whole Foods.

Greg is also a public speaker and panelist with expertise in producing for social change, alternative energy, and transformative thought. His speaking engagements include: Aspen Renewable Energy Summit, David Lynch Masters Film Program, Fordham University, Julia Ann Wrigley Global Institute of Sustainability, Sundance Film Festival, and United Nations. Greg Reitman received his BA at the University of Massachusetts at Amherst. He is a member of the Director's Guild of America. He currently resides in Los Angeles, living a green lifestyle.

GREG REITMAN

ROOTED IN
PEACE

AN INSPIRING STORY OF
FINDING PEACE WITHIN

Llewellyn Publications
Woodbury, Minnesota

FIRST EDITION
First Printing, 2018

Cover design by Kevin R. Brown
Editing by Brian R. Erdrich

Llewellyn Publications is a registered trademark of Llewellyn Worldwide Ltd.

Library of Congress Cataloging-in-Publication Data
Names: Reitman, Greg, author.
Title: Rooted in peace : an inspiring story of finding peace within / Greg
   Reitman.
Description: First edition. | Woodbury, Minnesota : Llewellyn Publications,
   [2018].
Identifiers: LCCN 2018022611 (print) | LCCN 2018030748 (ebook) | ISBN
   9780738755694 (ebook) | ISBN 9780738754024 | ISBN 9780738754024q(alk. pa-
per)
Subjects: LCSH: Peace of mind. | Peace—Psychological aspects.
Classification: LCC BF637.P3 (ebook) | LCC BF637.P3 R56 2018 (print) | DDC
   158.1—dc23
LC record available at https://lccn.loc.gov/2018022611

Llewellyn Worldwide Ltd. does not participate in, endorse, or have any authority or responsibility concerning private business transactions between our authors and the public.

All mail addressed to the author is forwarded, but the publisher cannot, unless specifically instructed by the author, give out an address or phone number.

Any internet references contained in this work are current at publication time, but the publisher cannot guarantee that a specific location will continue to be maintained. Please refer to the publisher's website for links to authors' websites and other sources.

Llewellyn Publications
A Division of Llewellyn Worldwide Ltd.
2143 Wooddale Drive
Woodbury, MN 55125.2989
www.llewellyn.com

Printed in the United States of America

To Britta, for opening my heart.

Contents

INTRODUCTION

The highest form of intelligence is being, the highest
form of feeling is love, the highest form of thinking is
creativity, and the highest form of doing is service.

—DEEPAK CHOPRA

Trees. They have many branches, yet every branch starts from
one root. Trees are nearly everywhere, and wherever they are
not—arctic tundra, blistering desert, urban concrete, or steel lab-
yrinth—the land is barren and inhospitable to life. Without trees,
we might as well be on the moon. If we value ourselves, we must
value trees. They are the force that puts us in balance.

Trees are a metaphor for humanity. We come from many
faiths, ethnicities, nationalities; we speak many languages and
worship different gods. Our world is as divided as it is diverse;
unresolved conflicts, wars, and numerous armed struggles still
haunt so many people and nations, cultures, and religions. Yet

in the end, we are all the same; we grow from the same root. We live, we breathe, we eat, we love, we learn, we work; we yearn for balance, meaning, and a higher purpose before we die. We strive for peace. And we all face the same problems—ecological disaster, continuous global war, inner turmoil. Trees ask us to examine how we live in the natural world—with one another and intrapersonally. If we value ourselves, we value trees. They are the force that puts us in balance.

Based on my documentary *ROOTED in PEACE*, this book challenges readers to examine their values as Americans and human beings. Today we are at war within ourselves, with our environment, and with the world. Gradually, we have come to be consumed by fear. In the documentary *ROOTED in PEACE*, I posit that this cycle of violence and retaliation must end. And it can end. Sadly, most people and cultures don't change unless they go through suffering and pain. But there is another way. We must get out of this reptilian sensibility—us versus them, survival versus nonexistence—and evolve to a higher state full of love and compassion. If it is possible for all of us to live in a society based on individual freedom, where the priority is always our common good, then there is hope. The story of *ROOTED in PEACE* is an adventure in seeking that starting point, one where peace takes root. Indeed, I don't just see this as "my journey." Rather, this is a journey of "we" in which each of us invests in preserving the enormity of life and the well-being of our planet. We all have within ourselves our own yearnings for peace. We are all citizens of the globe and stakeholders in this process.

As I began my search for the roots of peace, I realized that I couldn't change the world by myself. Who am I, after all? A typical Gen-Xer brought up in a small suburb of New York who had the opportunity to attend college and become educated. Besides, I am just one small person among billions. What possible impact could I have on the world as a whole? It was when I realized my quest wasn't mine alone but one I could share that *ROOTED in PEACE* first began to take shape as a concept and an ideal.

As a documentary filmmaker and Sundance Film Festival alumnus, I witnessed the impact of the commercial release of my film *FUEL* on society at-large. Tens of thousands of mothers and others—moved by the film's message—walked out of screening rooms and theaters and immediately moved to sell their SUVs, replacing them with hybrids. We did that. With images on a screen. We showed the world the ease with which fuel replacements were accessible and how important the need for that transition was, and suddenly we had an effect. Who ever would have ever imagined that Toyota would become the car manufacturer to lead us in saving the environment? But their hybrids and electric vehicles have led the way to an entire industry of mass-produced carbon-neutral options, and families everywhere are now choosing humanity over vanity.

If I could create a film and book that would help the environment, I reasoned, I could also make one that would enable people to become aware of themselves as citizens of this planet. Perhaps the film could alter human behavior and help us all make better choices in other collective areas of human experience. Maybe it would even foster peace. What would our world be like then?

I was around twelve years old, attending Hebrew School at Temple Beth Torah, when I was first introduced to the sacred duty of planting trees. Many years later, while attending college at the University of Massachusetts in Amherst, I returned to the practice and began planting peace trees—introducing a program I now call "One Tree"—that is dedicated to self-empowerment and environmental stewardship. But it wasn't until after 9/11 that I decided to create a documentary and accompanying book entitled *Rooted in Peace* to record my search for inner and outer peace—a search in which I met countless peace activists, politicians, environmentalists, media moguls, scientists, and spiritual advisors who continued to encourage me forward on this journey. Each one has connected me with others on the same path. But this is not a private, self-absorbed mission à la *Eat, Pray, Love*. As I strive to understand the realities we face, as I question world leaders and innovative thinkers, I challenge all of us to examine our values as Americans and as human beings. Regardless of how you identify yourself, this collective journey is on all our shoulders.

Today we are at war within ourselves, with our environment, and with the world. Gradually, even unconsciously, we have come to be consumed by fear and driven by our strict adherence to our identities. I want us to take notice, stop the cycle of violence, and proactively seek ways to find personal and geopolitical balance. The documentary and this book draw from memoir interspersed with interviews of luminaries and activists such as: former Vice President Al Gore; former President of Costa Rica Jose Maria Figueres; Nobel Peace Laureates Mairead

Maguire and Archbishop Desmond Tutu; Deepak Chopra; music legends Donovan, Mike Love, and Pete Seeger; film director David Lynch; media magnate Ted Turner; Joe Cirincione, Founder of the Ploughshares Fund; Jodie Evans, co-founder of CODEPINK; neuropsychiatrist Dan Siegel; MacArthur fellow and world-renowned environmentalist Lester Brown; William McDonough, author of *Cradle to Cradle*; Paul Hawken; oceanographer Fabien Cousteau; CEO of Patagonia Casey Sheahan; and many others. Throughout, I heed the words of Maharishi Mahesh Yogi, "If the forest is to be green, every tree must be green. If there's going to be peace on earth, then everybody must feel that quality of peace."

The experts I interacted with served as guides for me, helping me redefine my character. It is my deepest desire that my encounters with these remarkable people will guide you too. Among the most profound lessons I learned was that in order to change the world I would have to change myself first—and that meant looking inwardly. As Deepak Chopra told me, "If you really want to create peace in the world then you can't be angry, not even as a peace activist." My journey has allowed me to understand the power of love as a driving force for good—love for the earth, love of oneself, and love for the people in my life.

And so I pose this basic question, and in this book I ask you to do the same. Take a moment. Think about it. *How do you want to live?* In fear and conflict or free and in peace? We've all heard Mahatma Gandhi's imperative to "be the change that you wish to see in the world." And so, in asking readers to do the same—to ask themselves this most basic of questions: "*How do we want to live?"*—I'm hoping to begin a collective search for the answer. I believe that when we all begin to focus on that question, then we have planted the seed from which the roots of peace will grow.

Sparking a personal quest to understand human consciousness, *Rooted in Peace* provokes readers to return to balance within themselves, among humankind, and in the natural world. It awakens them to a more peaceful reality and asks them to find the ways and means to fulfill their deep desire: to live in a world filled with love and compassion for all life. A world rooted in peace. I take you along on my journey so that you can be informed by my encounters with people deeply engaged in the quest for peace at all levels. Indeed, this is a memoire of personal transformation through the lens of my yearning for a better world. But I am not special. I believe my experience is the human experience. I've struggled to make meaning of the chaotic world around me. By following my footsteps, you may find ideas and tools to help you in your own evolution toward a more peaceful self. If enough of us undertake this journey, perhaps we will engender a paradigm shift—that is my hope, anyway.

LOSING AND
FINDING OUR WAY

You cannot fix the world. You can only fix yourself, and
that is hard enough.

—DEEPAK CHOPRA

At the age of nineteen I was trying to figure out my life, and I
found myself in the middle of a war.

The first Gulf War.

At four a.m. I was standing on a ladder, picking avocados
at Kibbutz Gesher in the Beit She'an Valley in northern Israel.
I'd been in Israel for three months and had already become ac-
customed to this kind of physical labor, happy to be paid one

dollar a day for the opportunity to reevaluate my life away from the noise and pressures at home.

At six a.m. sirens sounded. Rather than going to breakfast, I was issued a gas mask. Out of the corner of my eye I saw an Arab Muslim woman pull a mask over her child's face. For an instant I wondered how she would explain to her little girl why she needed to wear such a thing, but then I was herded into a bomb shelter along with other foreign volunteers and a group of Russian immigrants. We all sat there listening to the muffled blare of the siren, not knowing what was going on or when we would be allowed to come out. Sure, we were aware that Saddam Hussein had invaded Kuwait and that the US had responded, but it wasn't until I first put on that gas mask that the war came home to me. The hiss of my breath and the way the goggles shaped my vision brought the war right to my face— up close and personal. Hussein was firing scud missiles at Israel. We feared biological warfare and poison gas. We knew he was capable of such heinous acts even against his own people. This was not a joke. It was really happening.

All of the concrete shelter's windows and doors were sealed. We were locked in. Imprisoned for the sake of our own safety. I sounded and looked like Darth Vader in that breathing contraption. I wasn't allowed to take it off. I wasn't allowed to get out of the bunker. I didn't know if I would ever get out. I became claustrophobic. Panic. Mental terror beyond imagination. How do I protect myself? My skin? I was just a kid from a small suburban town just outside of New York City who'd lost his way during his freshman year at college and taken off six months to find himself. I wasn't trained to fight, to deal with this insanity. I wasn't ready to die. I'd hardly even begun my life.

My Israeli friends at the Kibbutz had all vanished—called up in the middle of the night, they left to join their army regiments without a word of farewell. I had no one to talk to, no one who would reassure me. It was just us foreigners in the shelter, and I felt completely alone among them.

I thought about the Arab Muslim mother and her child, and a memory floated back to me. I am five years old. I am in my front yard holding a wooden stick and a plastic bag, walking toward the sewer to go fishing and catch the "Big Fish." Out of nowhere, a car pulls out from the driveway. Quickly, I try to move out of the way only to be struck by the car. It crushes my leg. As the ambulance drives us off to the hospital, an oxygen mask is placed over my face. In the dimness of the shelter, the scene came back to me vividly. My mother's screams. The sirens. The pain. The mask. I kept asking myself, "How does a mother explain to her child why she needs to wear a mask?"

I observed my compatriots. An eighteen-year-old girl from Florida, red-haired and freckled, became hysterical, hyperventilating. She went into shock, unwilling or unable to put on her mask. She had to be carried out. The Russians were frozen in terror. If this was going to end well, and I was to actually walk out of the shelter in one piece, I had options. I could go home. But they had no choice. They couldn't go back to the country that had persecuted them. I watched their fear and consternation—having abandoned one deathtrap only to find themselves stranded in another. A sad irony.

No bombs fell that day. Not on our kibbutz, anyway. After about an hour the sirens stopped. I emerged, blinking, into the bright sunshine. The low buildings and avocado groves stood untouched. I removed my mask and inhaled deeply. It was over—for now.

But was it really?

I returned to New York, and as Operation Desert Storm wound down, things began to normalize in Israel. During the ensuing months I returned back to Israel, enrolling at Tel Aviv University, where I regained my bearings as a student. But even as I dove into my coursework I couldn't get the memory of that mother and child out of my mind. The girl was the one I'd watched most while we were in the shelter. I had tried to read her face but I couldn't see it through the mask. Did being a child shield her in some way because she was too young to understand this danger? Or would this terrifying hour become a dull tone at the bottom of her heart, forever affecting the way she took in the world?

Later, when the fear from that day in the bomb shelter rose up inside me, I would talk myself out of it. In the hierarchy of trauma mine was not a big one, and I chided myself for still feeling it so deeply and being unable to let it go. Who was I to consider myself traumatized when soldiers were at war? Men and women were running into gunfire, having their limbs blown off daily, and all I had endured was sitting in a dark room with a few hundred people while wearing a gas mask. Besides, it hadn't scared me that much. It's not like I returned to the States and refused to ever leave again. I still yearned to see much more of the world, and studying in Tel Aviv was just the beginning.

Eventually, I found my way back to the University of Massachusetts at Amherst, back in the safe surroundings of the East Coast of the United States. But before long I was off again. I discovered an extraordinary summer program at Hokkaido University in Sapporo, Japan. Once there I traveled with several classmates to Hiroshima. We visited Peace Memorial Park, which stands on what had once been a busy part of town, before the first atom bomb destroyed everything within a five-mile radius. At the museum we saw footage taken before the bomb went off, destroying this neighborhood. People were walking casually down the street, mothers with their children darting in and out of the shops, the regular life of a city. The bomb killed more than 129,000 people on that August day near the end of World War II … in an instant.

With those images in mind, we stood looking at the park's peace monument, the ghostly ruin of the Hiroshima Prefectural Industrial Promotion Hall. The iron rods that supported that dome had withstood the atomic blast, but they seemed fragile against the sky and under the weight of our feelings. We lingered in front of the Statue of Mother and Child in the Storm, which depicts a woman bent over to shield her baby from the radioactive blast while an older child grabs onto her back. She could protect only one or the other, but not both. My friends wept in front of this sculpture, but to my surprise, no tears for me. Why didn't I cry?

I was dumbfounded. Numb. The mother's instinctual response depicted in the statue echoed that of the mother in the bomb shelter who moved quickly to place the gas mask on her child first. Those two images stood side-by-side in my mind, but seemed not to move my heart. And that made me think that something was not right. I should be reacting to this, but I'm not. "What's wrong with me?" I kept asking myself. I couldn't tell anyone, and I couldn't figure it out.

Two weeks later, I returned to UMASS Amherst for the fall semester. One month into school, I awakened in the middle of the night, trembling. I'd had a nightmare. I was sweating profusely, and my face was wet with tears. I had been traumatized by my experiences in Israel and Japan, and it was all starting to emerge. The terror, the sick feeling in my stomach, it was all coming back to me. I was unaware then, but I had been holding on to post-traumatic stress, and now it was bubbling out.

I sat at the edge of my bed, thinking about how I'd been devastated by the effects of the Gulf War coupled with my new understanding of the consequences of a nuclear bomb. But although I was shaken, I now also felt released in some way. My emotions had been dulled by these powerful occurrences, and I'd expended energy to muffle their impact. After this darkness washed through me, I knew I was free to feel, and free to engage with the world.

Suddenly, I felt that I needed to act, to do something. I felt an overwhelming need to make a difference, to have an impact, to find a purpose. I came up with the crazy idea that I would plant trees to save the world. I was on a mission. I looked to Al

Gore's book *Earth in Balance* as an inspiration. He was my hero. I would organize a tree drive on my UMASS Amherst campus called "The Giving Tree: Rooted in Peace."

WHY TREES?

I probably wouldn't have been able to tell you then. But now, I've come to realize that trees can be a metaphor for humanity. They have many branches, but every branch reaches out from one trunk. We all manifest from the same roots. If we start there, perhaps we can find a commonality that could change the world.

But no one got my message then, or perhaps I hadn't understood it well enough to articulate it clearly to my fellow students. My quest collapsed even before it began. Fellow students mocked my proposals; religious groups on campus were outraged; my own father failed to appreciate my cause. It was as if people had become more comfortable in a world where there was conflict, or at least uncomfortable if they did not make conflict the center of their daily thoughts. Later, when I and others tried to plant a tree in New York City, we discovered it was more expensive and complicated than it was to buy a gun. It seemed to me that we were not only at war with ourselves, but with our environment and with the world. No wonder my plea to come together to plant trees as a symbol of peace was met with such derision.

I accepted defeat, and for many years I let this idea lay fallow.

Then, a decade later, I found myself reliving the horrors of war—this time in my hometown of New York City. My sister and loved ones lived in Lower Manhattan, a quarter of a mile from the World Trade Center. My little niece attended preschool just three hundred feet from the towers. The 9/11 bombings sent fear throughout the globe and especially into every American living room as we watched on TV over and over again how the second plane crashed into the building and those towers came down.

And it retraumatized me.

THE BIRTH OF A FILM

After the success of my first commercial documentary film *FUEL*, when I considered what I wanted to look into next, I thought about my derailed quest for peace. I still wanted it and still worked for it. I had been involved in peace demonstrations through the reaction to 9/11. I had opposed our country's military misadventures since that terrorist attack, but this too was a lonely and painful road. The world was moving further and further away from peace, and the number of people who sought it appeared to be dwindling. When I looked at my life experience since that idealistic epiphany in college, I wanted more than ever to explore ways to focus the world's attention on the need for peace.

But where does the average person begin? Who am I, after all? I'm not Desmond Tutu. I'm one among many Gen-Xers brought up in a small suburb, just another idealistic college grad. I decided that the place to begin was to do what I usually do: I started asking questions.

I began my search for peace by looking at the world's conflicts, and reached out to dozens of luminaries, thinkers, writers, and activists—those whose work for peace had garnered international attention and awards. My success as a fellow Sundance award-winning documentary filmmaker gave me the courage, access, and credibility to speak with experts the average person couldn't easily approach—allowing me to interview people such as Ted Turner, William McDonough, Lester Brown, Dr. Mark Hyman, Deepak Chopra, singers Pete Seeger, Donovan, and Mike Love of the Beach Boys, film director and writer David Lynch, Nobel Peace Laureate Mairead Maguire of Ireland, and countless others.

I learned much about the extraordinary level of violence in our world, injuries that hit us from so many directions at once. Indeed, it is no wonder we have become dulled to it in order to get through our days. With each conversation, I saw more of the many dimensions of this problem and became more discouraged. It was overwhelming.

Millions have become refuges under perilous circumstances, fleeing their homes where conditions have become unbearable and a brutal death is a near certainty. Just a light glance at the world around could overwhelm us, and here I was immersing myself in it.

The feeling of peace is something we want earnestly deep in our hearts, but when faced with the decision to be peaceful, to walk in peace, to greet the world with love, we leap back, go numb, shut and lock the door. Why? Because we live in a world of instant media delivery. The devastation of a tsunami in Japan comes to us as swiftly, and as vividly, as the massacre of children in their elementary school in Connecticut. These images are almost as traumatizing to us observers as they are to those directly involved. That's what experts refer to as secondhand trauma. The paradox is that our universal and continual electronic connection to one another has actually isolated us and rendered us even more fearful.

And so, against our will, we have been sucked into the trauma vortex.

WHAT IS THE TRAUMA VORTEX?

Think of a whirlpool in which an act of violence perpetrated against innocent people causes collective trauma, which then breeds rage and retaliation on the part of the victims, which then breeds trauma on the other side, which then breeds their rage and retaliation in an endlessly descending spiral of hatred and dehumanization, retribution and mutual destruction.

Los Angeles trauma expert and psychotherapist Gina Ross explains the wider implications of the trauma vortex. "Unhealed trauma is not static," she told me. "It keeps augmenting; it keeps amplifying. And so, from something that just made a small part of your life dysfunctional, it can spread to a bigger and bigger part of your life, and then the lives of the people around you, and then your community." The metaphor of the trauma vortex (as coined by Dr. Peter Levine) is expressive of its dynamic nature—this impulsive energy that keeps growing like a virus of pain and suffering and dysfunction.

Many people do not recognize the role of trauma in their lives. They believe that they feel bad because feeling bad is a logical response to events. Feeling bad feels right. Inside that worldview, we have no peace. We are already dead—closed off to the beauty and preciousness of life.

The more I learned from the peace scholars whom I interviewed, the more I realized that I needed to expand my definition of peace. I had thought of it as the cessation of conflict, and by that I meant world conflict, but when I talked about the trauma vortex with Dr. Deepak Chopra, he described peace in a way that led me toward a completely new understanding.

SEEKING PEACE CONSCIOUSNESS

"Peace is a state of consciousness where it becomes impossible to hurt or be hurt," Dr. Chopra told me. "When you are perfectly established in peace consciousness, all beings around you cease to feel hostility no matter what the situation, circumstance, event, or person around you. You cannot be shaken from that unassailable state of being totally in peace, in bliss, in happiness, and in truth. I think peace is very contagious and peace is very powerful."

Contagious and powerful? Dr. Chopra expressed exactly the opposite of what I had experienced. But that's because he didn't see the quest for peace played out on an international stage. Isolated efforts were well-intentioned and admirable, but ultimately he felt they were futile and almost beside the point. "You cannot fix the world," he told me. "You can only fix yourself, and that is hard enough."

With our feet set in fear and suspicion, traumatized by our pasts, we remain hunkered down in a constant state of vigilance. But when I saw peace through Dr. Chopra's eyes, I understood the truth behind the lyrics of the song "Let There Be Peace on Earth." Looking into my own heart, I recognized that I was not a peaceful soul. No. I was angry. Much about what was happening in the world enraged me. Many political discussions started off reasonably enough, but soon they turned into rants. The world had to change and so did most of the people running it. Didn't people know this? What was wrong with them? Couldn't they see the world the way I did?

We can march for peace, donate to charities that advocate for it, and vote for politicians who say that they value a more peaceful world, but in my view there were various forces arrayed against peace. I saw how frustrating it was to try to bring peace to a traumatized society, whose membership included me. In the end, I grew to understand that the search for peace begins a lot closer to home.

This is where ROOTED in PEACE takes a turn from an exploration of our violent and traumatized world to an internal quest and a love story. My journey to peace turned to the functioning of the brain and heart as well as a better understanding of the survival instincts that motivate many of our actions. The truth is, a sizeable portion of our responses are governed by our reptilian brain, the section that sees the world as good or evil. Are you a benefit or a threat to me? And the margins around that decision-making are very thin. This is why, with all the rejection and ridicule I'd faced in my initial quest for peace, I had become more reptilian, more defensive, more prone to seeing enemies first, and less convinced that I had any allies. This oppositional stance affected many of my interactions with the world, and especially the most important ones with my now wife, Britta.

ROOTED in PEACE is the story of my quixotic quest to open my own heart to peace. We see peace as something that we must achieve together by brave conscious agreements to lay down our weapons and open our arms. That same courageous approach is the way to find peace within: to have compassion for our failings and forgive ourselves for all the pain we have caused others, and others for the pain they have brought us. In many ways, the inward journey has even stronger opponents than my quest to bring peace to the world, as it required me to address the dysfunction in my life, the only part of the world I had any control over. Most of us don't want to go inside. Our minds will give us a hundred reasons why we can't do it, and we are easily convinced not to try, because in doing so it allows us to avoid this difficult inner work.

I know I battled myself at every turn along the way. I didn't come from a family of peaceniks. Rather, like many of us, my parents were first-generation Americans whose grandparents came from Europe. Their primary focus was finding work, putting food on the table, and ensuring that both my sister and I had the opportunity to attend college and make a better life for ourselves. Questions relating to peace and inner conflict were not the norm at the dinner table. Though my grandfather was a war veteran serving in World War II, when I talked to my mom about my serving in the Air Force, she quietly denied my aspirations, saying, "We didn't raise you to be a soldier of war, but rather a lawyer or a doctor." Consequently, the demons inside my head were a lot louder than the small, gentle voices advocating for peace.

So, in order to make progress, I worked on processing my trauma through the body, getting healthy, eating well, and—at last—meditating regularly to calm and balance my mind. This book details the changes I made in my habits and how those led to my self-transformation and my interactions with the world.

As I changed the face I presented to the world, the world began to present a different face to me. My perceptions had been occluded until I took off my mask and breathed the pure, clean air of peace.

Through it all, the one who stood by my side, tolerated my excesses, and cheered me on as I progressed was Britta. The constant and sustaining love that always emanated from her was the strongest beacon guiding this journey. She is the kind of person who loves effortlessly, or so it seemed to me, and always unconditionally. She wanted the best for me so much that she found a way to handle my worst. When I calmed the dirty demons within that had been guiding my actions, it was then I felt peace and I was able to love her back. Then I was able to ask her if she would do me the honor of being my wife.

Peace and love, the cliché pairing from the hippies of the 1960s, doesn't seem so clichéd to me now. They are a matched set and harder to experience than many who say them so lightly could imagine. Yet they are possible to bring about by focusing one's attention on the kinds of habits and practices that bring them into existence in daily life. Lest you think that all of this is a completely self-absorbed self-regard and of no use to the many problems of the world, I bring you back to the words of

Dr. Chopra, who pointed out that while I could not change the world, changing the self was hard enough.

ROOTED IN PEACE: THE BOOK

I have written *Rooted in Peace: An Inspiring Story of Finding Peace Within* as a companion to my documentary film of the same name. Here, I follow a similar trajectory as I seek to understand the meaning of peace—politically, interpersonally, and intrapersonally. In films, ideas and images pass by quickly, vanishing into the darkness of the theater. With a book in hand, you will be able to stop and contemplate how my questions and search could apply to your own life.

I take you along on my journey so that you can be informed by my encounters with people deeply engaged in the quest for peace at all levels. Indeed, this is a memoire of personal transformation through the lens of my yearning for a better world. But I am not special. I believe my experience is the human experience. By following my footsteps, you may find ideas and tools to help you in your own evolution toward a more peaceful self. If enough of us undertake this journey, perhaps we will engender a paradigm shift—that is my hope, anyway.

The experts I interacted with served as guides for me, helping me redefine my character. It is my deepest desire that my encounters with these remarkable people will guide you too. Among the most profound lessons I learned was that in order to change the world, I would have to change myself first—and that meant looking inwardly. As Deepak Chopra told me, "If you really want to create peace in the world, then you can't be angry, not even as a peace activist." I also finally understood the power of love as a driving force for good—love for the earth, love of oneself, and love for the people in my life.

Most importantly, I discovered my connection to the world and every living thing in it. I discovered that the world is as I am. The world is as you are.

So … who are you?

GUNS AND ROSES

In our mind, we have this crazy idea—and I would love to know where it really comes from—that we can kill each other, that we can actually train people to kill each other.

—MAIREAD MAGUIRE, NOBEL PEACE LAUREATE

Omar Samaha, born in Fairfax, Virginia, graduated from Virginia Tech in 2006. When I met him he was twenty-seven years old.

"You know that saying, 'Virginia is for lovers'?" I asked Omar when I first met him. I wanted to know what it meant to him, but he really didn't have a clue.

"Virginia doesn't seem to have that loving culture," he replied. "I just don't see it that often. Virginia is pretty militaristic and government-like when it comes to the culture—very standard, by the books, old-school."

Omar had lots of friends in the military, or whose parents were in the military, or worked for the government. He considered joining the Air Force or the Marines, and mentioned in his college applications that he wanted to join the Air Force ROTC. That was before he decided to focus on soccer rather than join the armed forces. "I wanted to play soccer at the highest levels, as opposed to dropping bombs on people," he told me. This is not to say he was a young pacifist. "I used to play games with guns all the time," he admitted. "I have vivid memories of cops and robbers growing up and paintball in the backyard as I got older, and BB guns—it was common." Simulated gunplay is part of our culture. But then things changed the morning of April 16, 2007.

Omar woke up to his father walking into his room. Two people had been killed at Virginia Tech. Omar explained, "I figured it was just an isolated incident. I thought, 'Why are you waking me up to tell me this?' But as the day went on, I received a phone call from my dad. He was saying that people were getting shot all over campus. He was freaking out on the phone. I ended up going back home and trying to call my sister."

Reema was an eighteen-year-old freshman and an A-student, and she loved to dance. The Samaha family began receiving phone calls from relatives and friends around the world, asking whether Reema was okay. "We had no idea what happened to her because we couldn't get ahold of her," Omar said. "I finally heard from one of her friends that Reema was in the building where the shootings took place, but I didn't want to believe her. I wanted to think that she was just confined to a building to wait until things were taken care of, like, on lock-down. I knew buildings on campus were on lockdown. So, I held out hope that she was okay and just not able to talk on the phone yet. Or I thought that she was potentially injured, but in the hospital and getting help."

Reema had been in her French class at the time. Her class had seventeen students, and eleven were killed. But no information was relayed to the Samahas. They drove four hours from northern Virginia to Virginia Tech to find out that Reema, indeed, had been one of the victims. They heard unofficially from an ambulance driver. A school counselor corroborated the driver's account that Reema had died in the massacre. In terms of what happened that day, they never got official word from the school. It took weeks to piece together the story. They later learned that the shooter, Seung-Hui Cho, an alien-resident from Korea and senior at Virginia Tech, had been judged mentally ill. Suffering from delusions, he killed two people on campus early that morning and then escaped. He sent a video of testimony regarding his motives to a news agency in New York. He subsequently returned to campus, chained three exit doors shut in the Academic Building, and went from classroom to classroom, opening fire.

I asked Omar how he reacted when he got the news. "I had been in a room with my family waiting to hear if Reema was one of the victims," he told me. "My other sister and my mom left for a little bit. As I was sitting there with my father, someone came up to us and told us Reema had died. I told my dad, 'I don't want to tell Mom and Randa.' He said, 'We have to ...'

We sat there in silence and shock. When my mom and my sister came back, we got up to meet them at the doorway. We didn't have to say anything. Even though we weren't crying, they could just tell by the look on our faces. My mom and sister immediately broke down. They literally threw themselves on the ground. There was nothing you could do to stop any of us from crying at that point."

I was curious whether anyone had ever researched how Seung-Hui Cho had obtained the gun he used to commit this massacre—at the time, the deadliest mass murder perpetrated by a single gunman in US history. Omar told me that the police reports stated he had actually used two guns to kill thirty-two people and injured twenty-five more. He had bought them on separate occasions. That meant he had passed two National Instant Criminal System (NICS) background checks. "There's a list of prohibited purchasers in this country. In order to buy a gun, the seller has to run a background check to make sure you're not one of them. Seung-Hui Cho should never have cleared either check," Omar continued. "He passed only because his name wasn't entered into a national database."

Cho had obtained one of the weapons at a gun shop in Roanoke, close to Virginia Tech. He purchased the second gun online from a secondary store in another state. This was puzzling to me. I'd been looking into buying a gun to use as a prop for my documentary film, and I learned that it's illegal to buy one out-of-state. But where did that put online vendors—in some gray area? Yes.

This is also true for guns purchased at gun shows—what has become known as the "gun show loophole." Omar found that guns were the easiest thing to get at these shows. "It's just like buying a candy bar or a bag of chips from a convenience store," he told me. "I went undercover and bought ten guns in one hour at a Richmond gun show after April 16, just to see how easy it was," he explained. "No one asked me any questions—I didn't even have to show my ID. I just gave them cash, and they gave me a gun." The bottom line is if you have the money, you can buy a firearm. Omar even bought a Glock pistol in the parking lot outside the gun show for about $400.

That's not all. According to a recent editorial in the *New York Times*, a person on the FBI's terrorist watch list is barred from boarding an airplane but is free to buy a high-power weapon and ammunition at any American gun shop. The latest federal data shows that 272 individuals on the terrorist watch list tried to buy firearms in 2010 and all but twenty-five were cleared to make the purchase. (Those who were rejected had criminal records of felonies, spousal abuse, and other threats.)

In fact, I've found that it's harder to put a tree in the ground than it is to buy a gun, even during a national observance like the International Day of Peace. In 2008 I planted ten trees at Waldorf School campuses in California and Colorado. When I got to New York, I was asked to join the Brooklyn Waldorf School in a tree planting ceremony at a public park. Unfortunately, the Brooklyn school wasn't able to get through the New York Parks Department's red tape. They charge $2,500 to plant a tree in a public park. But it costs only $250 to buy a gun.

In reading a newsletter from *Mayors Against Illegal Guns,* an organization created by New York Mayor Michael Bloomberg, I was shocked to learn that thirty-four people around the country are killed by gunfire daily. Not surprisingly, after Omar's family discovered how easy it was for Seung-Hui Cho to obtain both guns, they became advocates for stricter gun control laws. They decided that the government needed to fix the background check system and to make sure that all the names of prohibited purchasers are put into the federal database. They also wanted to close the gun show loophole.

"We, as a society, have a lot of work to do when it comes to trying to prevent gun violence," Omar said. "Anyone can get a gun in this country. You could be adjudicated mentally ill, you could be a felon, you could be a terrorist, and you can still buy a gun without any questions asked."

As far as Omar knew, the Fairfax, Virginia–based National Rifle Association had little to say about the incident. In fact, after the massacre, splinter groups of the NRA decided that their way of dealing with the tragedy was to give more guns to more students. "They just tried to push guns on campus after that," Omar revealed. "They told a lot of students to carry guns to class, which is illegal. They wanted to change the law in Virginia. A group at Virginia Tech called 'Students for Concealed Carry on Campus' was actually pushing that." Some groups are even more extreme than the NRA. For instance, the Virginia Citizens Defense League advocates for fewer restrictions. As Omar explained, "If they had their way, there would be no restrictions on guns at all."

Understandably, Omar's feelings of safety in the world have been undermined. Not only that, he believes that no one should be complacent. "Gun violence affects everyone from all walks of life. It's a Virginia Tech tragedy every single day in this country. Just because the shootings are not located in a classroom building, or one centralized location, they are still happening every single day. A part of dealing with my trauma," said Omar, "is to prevent it from happening again. I don't want to see other families and friends go through what my family has gone through. The amount of pain that I witnessed makes me never want to see something like this happen to anyone ever again. It's hard for me to even think back to that day and remember exactly how things happened, because it's that painful. Trying to prevent violence helps me to deal with my trauma."

Omar found that a common thread links all people who have lost family members to gun violence. "It's the experience of going through something like that and losing someone, the pain that comes with it, and the need for action to try to stop it from happening again to others. People who haven't experienced gun violence, or trauma like this, might think they're immune, so they'd be hesitant to jump on board with us. But they need to in order to prevent it from happening to someone they know, or even themselves."

When I asked Omar how governmental officials reacted to the massacre, he told me that President George W. Bush visited the campus and made statements about various topics. But when it came to prevention, he didn't really speak much to that. "I don't think enough people spoke out from our government about what we need to do to prevent future tragedies. And since Virginia Tech, we've all seen more tragedies pop up across the country." Like the mass shooting in Tucson in which nineteen people were shot, six of them fatally. Indeed, even the Congressman representing Virginia Tech's congressional district did not support an initiative to prevent violence by closing the gun show loophole.

"There are so many victims of gun violence," Omar told me. "We meet these people, and they all have similar feelings towards the topic. Our lives were shattered in many different ways, and now we're trying to prevent the same thing from happening to others. Why wouldn't the common everyday American want to support that? So many people don't even know about the things that actually happen in this country, and the laws that exist, and the laws that we condone and live with every single day."

Why, indeed?

WE GROW UP THIS WAY

The answer seems to be that violence and war are part of our culture. Mark Gerzon, author and expert at the Mediators Foundation, which incubates projects supporting global peace, told me that the history of American manhood was shaped by the unique archetype of the *frontiersmen*—think Davy Crockett and Daniel Boone. "The French, Germans, Russians, they all have the soldier archetype. But in addition to the soldier, we have the frontiersman. That, put together with the soldier archetype, creates a culture that needs violence and war to prove its masculinity and its identity."

Gerzon even made the point that our culture *needs* war periodically. "If you look at American history when there were long periods without war, you would have men stand up and say, 'You know, we're getting soft here in America. We're getting soft and lazy and I feel we need to create. ...' Some of the energy around the Olympics and Outward Bound came out of looking for an alternative to war because we need it to prove our manhood. That's a very American idea, also a very European idea in some cultures. But if you go to Sri Lanka, or India, or any number of places around the world, you do not find people saying, 'Okay, son, for you to become a man you gotta go to war.' The energy is not there. It's not part of their culture."

Our American history books teach us about war. It is idolized in our school books, celebrated on our national holidays, and consumed in our pop culture in film and television. Author and Buddhist monk Lama Surya Das said even the popular movie actor John Wayne personifies this American cowboy male ego whether as a Green Beret, a pilot, or a fire chief. What about Rambo? Or our favorite Terminator, Arnold Schwarzenegger? Warlike figures have become our national identity. It's cool to go to war. It's cool to join the Marines. It's cool to blow people away. And worse, our youth believes this like it's a form of the gospel.

War culture is everywhere in our society; it's fed like cereal to our children. And yet, we have no awareness of what we're creating—a culture in which violence and power, but not peace, are considered the highest values. I, myself, was not immune to violent games or the violence here in America. Like Omar, I admit that I grew up firing a BB gun. It was standard procedure to play cops and robbers. I did the Cowboy-and-Indian routine with my friends and enjoyed war games on Atari. I, too, thought I was cool.

In an attempt to understand the pervasive nature of violence in our pop culture, I visited E3—the Electronic Entertainment Expo—the annual video game conference and tradeshow in Los Angeles. E3 is a four billion dollar marketplace that consists mostly of violent video games. In fact, if you spend any time there, you'll see that the video game industry promotes hard-core violence that pulsates into kids' brains and injects into their bloodstream the notion that virtual killing is acceptable—even fun.

The moment of truth for me came while I was standing in the middle of the noisy tradeshow floor. I was surrounded by beautiful girls wearing army fatigues or dressed up like World War II Fly Girls proselytizing war games. There were even booths with military men representing their service branches. They had been tasked with ensuring that the games were technically correct. For instance, I even had a chance to talk with a Navy officer who asked to be unnamed and he expressed to me that because most video games today are violent, he refuses to allow his eight-year-old to play them. But, on the other hand, when the kids who are age-appropriate learn how to play those games, they're having fun with them. Why not make it accurate? Why not put the correct weapon in the Navy Seal's hands?

Why not put him on the correct helicopter and do it right? Later he told me, "Some kids know more about weapons than I do because they play these games." I don't know if this is something to be proud of.

The people who were selling a World War II game, which they described as "really fun because you get to shoot things," refused to talk to me on camera. When I asked another war game marketer about his product (which was rated Mature), he told me it caters to people who like "first-person shooters." He went on to say, "It's a type of gameplay people enjoy." When I asked him about the game's design, he said, "You've got to start with what makes for a fun interactive experience … that's critical. When someone picks up our controller, are they going to have a good time with an intuitive experience that they can enjoy? If you can't deliver that, you can't deliver a game." *Enjoy* killing people? Even in a virtual world, everything about that seems wrong.

Lois, who was marketing a sports kit for Wii that included a gun—actually a sniper rifle—explained to me the rationale behind its inclusion. "We don't want to leave anyone out," she said. "It's all about making the gaming experience feel real." Well, not exactly. The rifle was white. When I questioned Lois about that, she said, "We did try to make them fairly lifelike, but we can't make them totally lifelike. There's a limit on some things because we don't want it to actually be like a gun. People do need to remember that it is a peripheral." In fact, she told me that a government regulation prohibits game developers from making their guns black.

War reenactments and violent video games merge fantasy and reality. As I roamed the halls of E3, I kept wondering what these kinds of activities trigger in the brains of young people who play them. Are our children disconnecting themselves from their hearts? Are they becoming machines who respond with violence without thinking about its consequences? I was reminded of my five-year-old nephew. He wants to become a Jedi knight. With his light saber flashing, he's ready to attack. But he doesn't realize the deeper meanings of the classic Star War films. One does not become a Jedi through violence, but rather by mastering the inner life force and one's reactive emotional nature, by learning to communicate with one's inner power, by feeling "The Force" or spirit that connects us all to each other and the universe. He's too young to understand this—but not too young to brandish the weapon.

Pretty soon, I felt like the philosopher Diogenes wandering the streets of ancient Greece, lamp in hand, looking for one honest man. There was no sense of any alternative. Just war, war, war! "Where are the peace games?" I started asking the marketers. They looked at me like I was crazy. "You know," I pressed, "like the story of Gandhi. How he stood up against the British Army when they came with their tanks, and yet he didn't fight. He just stood there. Or a game that would include getting pearls of wisdom from the Dalai Lama and Deepak Chopra and Desmond Tutu. Maybe we could throw in the Beatles when they met the Maharishi and they sought Enlightenment." No go.

In my opinion, the origins of these developers selling these games to children are non-cognizant and unaware of the impact they're having on our youth. As it stands, are we really thinking about the next generation's behavior toward guns? Power begets more power. Violence begets more violence. Is this the right way of living? Can we deal with the aftermath of this recklessness? Well of course there are a handful of nonviolent video games, however the real issue is that the gaming industry is overwhelmingly violent, and there's no check and balance within the industry to ensure that protocols of safety and proper brain function are being regulated.

As a boy, I was a fan of video games without realizing that the superheroes and supervillains wallowed in blood and darkness. I sought out thought leaders on how much the hero archetype affects our perspective as we grow. Lama Surya Das talked to me about how these characters are "invulnerable, rather than vulnerable and sensitive." They don't kill, but are powerful, forceful, and unyielding rather than compassionate toward their enemies. And yet these character traits are how we program our youth. Are these the values we want to teach our youngsters?

I investigated the E3 show, continuing to look for peace games among the carnage—but I found none. Indeed, the people I interviewed were so deeply enmeshed in the culture of violence they were hawking, they seemed oblivious to the irony of my questions. As one saleswoman told me, while she described a war game now available on an iPhone app, "It's a fun game because you get to shoot things. I always like to shoot things."

Nobel Peace Laureate Mairead Maguire told me, "We have to start in our mind. In our mind, we have this crazy idea that we can kill each other." And the fact is, we do.

WAR

I'm not thinking anyone is going to deliberately blow up the world, but we've already got all the dynamite right here, loaded and ready to go. We're one button-push from blowing the whole place up.

—TED TURNER

"War is good business," says Joe Cirincione, president of the Ploughshares Fund (think "swords to ploughshares" from the Bible), a global security foundation that focuses on providing grants to projects that reduce and eliminate nuclear weapons. He told me, "Any country that can make airplanes thinks about making airplanes to kill other people. It's business. There's a market for this. Can you sell more of these? Well, you can if there's conflict."

Joe had been engaged in crafting nuclear weapons policy in Washington for twenty-five years. At first, he was on the oversight staff of the House Armed Services Committee, managing the programs to make sure they were running smoothly. This closer look gave him a different perspective on the nuclear arms issue. "I couldn't help looking at these programs," he told me, "and realizing that 1) this was *the* most destructive force humankind has ever made; 2) we had *way* too many of these things; 3) there was a lot of money being made on these bombs; and 4) a lot of the reason they still existed was because people were manipulating fear to make money and to keep the nuclear weapons complex alive, and that we weren't in control of this."

While Cirincione was on the staff of the House Armed Services Committee, he frequently met with executives of defense corporations. "These are not evil people," he told me. "They believe that what they are doing is in the patriotic interest of the country, and if they are making a little money off of it, well, that's business. But I have never met a defense contractor who lost a night's sleep over what they were doing. They believe in it. As far as they're concerned, this is America's business. This is America's security and they are getting rich off of it."

Nevertheless, there is a growing consensus in this and other countries that nuclear warheads are obsolete twentieth-century weapons. Leading world thinkers are all starting to believe that whatever security benefits nuclear weapons may have had are outweighed by their liabilities. We have to get rid of them. And that sentiment does not just come from people like me who oppose war. It's also coming from the very center of the American security establishment. "People who built the nuclear empire," Cirincione told me, "are now saying it's time to take it down. People like Henry Kissinger, and George Shultz, and Bill Perry, and Sam Nunn, and Colin Powell, and many, many former generals and admirals are saying, 'We don't need this anymore. We need the money for something else. And as long as these things are around, they're a threat to our national integrity.'"

And to some extent they are being heard. There are fewer nuclear weapons in the world now than there were twenty-five years ago or even last year. Despite the threats from Iran and North Korea, fewer countries have or are trying to get them, and more have given up these programs over the last thirty years than have tried to develop them. "When you look at the arc of history," Cirincione continued, "it is bending in our direction." Almost every country in the world has joined the Non-Proliferation Treaty; 183 of those nations don't have nuclear weapons and believe no one should. All fifteen members of the UN Security Council recently voted to rid the world of nuclear weapons. The vast majority of the world has already abandoned the idea of them. So why haven't we?

When I asked Joe that question, he replied, "Politics, inertia, and bureaucracy. If you want to reduce nuclear weapons, you get portrayed by your political opponents as weak, as an appeaser, as somebody who's giving away America's national security. You have to be careful about how you do this. You also have to move the bureaucracy. Even people who agree with you in the Pentagon have a bureaucracy of people whose lives and careers and officer billets depend on keeping that nuclear weapons complex just the way it is. When President Obama was negotiating the new START Treaty, he was visited by senators whose states had ICBM bases. There are 450 ICBMs in the United States scattered over ten states, and those senators said, 'Don't touch our ICBMs. They mean jobs for us.' Jobs. Jobs, not security. And then, of course, you have the people who make money off of this. They tell you that the ICBMs are wearing out and we need new ones. The bombers are wearing out. We need new ones." And once a defense contract is signed, it's extremely difficult to stop production.

Not only do these armaments endanger all of us, but they are an expensive proposition, draining our budget of funds that could be used for more life-enhancing endeavors. The truth is, today our nation devotes about a trillion dollars a year to all military-related programs, including our ongoing wars, veterans' benefits, and the interest we pay on the debt we incur in order to fight those wars. Of this, the United States spends $54 billion annually on nuclear weapons and weapons-related programs. We do that year after year, and these figures don't include new projects. For instance, a new generation of bombers, submarines, and missiles are just entering the manufacturing pipeline. They are going to cost us an additional $300 billion over the next ten years in addition to the $7.3 trillion dollars we're planning on spending over the next ten years on defense. Yes, the numbers are staggering. So why do we do this when these weapons are no longer necessary?

WAR IS GOOD BUSINESS

War is good business, right? Wrong. President Eisenhower himself, the war-hero general who contributed to our victory in World War II, warned about the reach of the military-industrial complex. As peace activist Jodie Evans said, "If we don't tell the stories of what war does, and how long it's been doing it, if we don't talk about what it feels like, then we carry it forward."

Like me, world-renowned green architect William McDonough visited Hiroshima. But he was much younger. "I remember holding my parents' hands," he told me, "and wondering why I was there. My parents were silent. They just said, 'You should see this.' How did Hiroshima disappear? Why did it disappear? I'm trying to understand why humans did this." Every president from Truman forward has engaged in the language of atomic warfare. Even former president Barack Obama said, "If we fail to act, we will invite nuclear arms races in every region and the prospect of wars and acts of terror on a scale that we can hardly imagine."

We are toying with the most destructive force that mankind has ever unleashed. As Ted Turner told me, "I'm not thinking anyone is going to deliberately blow up the world, but we've already got all the dynamite right here—loaded and ready to go. We're one button-push from blowing the whole place up."

Just imagine someone unstable waking up angry one morning and deciding to test a nuclear warhead. Pretty nuts. In their defense, the North Korean news agency said their 2009 test had been "safely conducted on a new higher level in terms of its explosive power and technology of its control... The test will contribute to defending the sovereignty of the country and the nation and socialism and ensuring peace and security on the Korean peninsula and the region."

As a species we have to ask ourselves if it makes sense to have nuclear bombs. Have we not learned from the Cold War? Isn't this an endgame? What purpose does it serve to sacrifice our health and education to nuclear weapons? Where is the balance? Why do we continue to do this to ourselves?

Conflict occurs when disparate parties who have differing views clash with one another. It's actually a natural part of the human experience and can be either positive or negative. If we approach conflict constructively, it can be an engine for growth and transformation. But as we have seen, if conflict devolves to violence, that only begets more violence. More often than not, it destroys lives and spirals into increased discord.

Author and peace activist Phillip Hellmich, senior officer at the Shift Network, told me that conflict is like a rainbow, but the pots of gold at either end are extreme decisions. Extreme decisions in a conflict will drive the agenda. Those who have the loudest voices and use anger and fear drive the agenda. We see that here in America with the polarization of Democrats and Republicans. When there's fear, we start to narrow our identity. "I'm a Conservative; you're a Liberal." "I'm Muslim; you're a Christian; you're a Jew." "I'm a Hindu; you're a Buddhist." And then the people who make those extreme decisions will start to confuse the issues and demonize the other rather than solve the problem at hand. It's a slippery slope of consciousness from there. It's always a zero-sum game with war, because someone loses and someone wins. But when you think about it, who really *wins*?

William J. Rouhana, Jr. the chairman and CEO of Chicken Soup for the Soul LLC, and the co-founder of the Humpty Dumpty Institute, tells us that war has a "hangover effect" which we often don't consider in terms of the psychological trauma and the stress it creates. We don't tend to focus on war's impact—that we leave countries so scarred that it prevents warring factions from reuniting.

Think about the hangover war leaves on a society. You're either a killer, or someone you love has been killed, a Shiite or a Sunni, a Muslim or a Christian, a Tutsi or a Hutu. Is this a great place to start from if you're trying to rebuild your society, your life? William J. Rouhana, Jr. phrases it best: "It's about putting the pieces back together. We see the world as highly fractured and in deep need of repair. And wherever we went, there were just so many problems. As the nursery rhyme says, 'All the King's horses and all the King's man couldn't put Humpty Dumpty back together again.'" How many times did we sing this ditty mindlessly as children? Yet it's a great source of inspiration now when you think about how it can apply to war and warriors. Even our own soldiers fighting in foreign lands are not immune. The divorce and suicide rates among returning Iraq and Afghan war vets is astronomical.

Serious and sustained conflict always involves dehumanizing the other. We can't kill people unless we've reduced them to subhumans, as was done in Rwanda and Iraq and Bosnia. When you call people insects, dogs, vermin, apes, or pigs, it's easier to murder them. You feel less guilt—after all, they don't deserve to live. Hitler did this with supreme efficiency to the Jews and others during the Holocaust.

Rouhana recalls his firsthand experiences in Rwanda. "No one could look you in the eye. No one could look anyone in the eye. They were either in mourning or consumed with guilt. I have never seen anything like this before. And I'd never seen it so pervasive across an entire society." Consciousness shuts down. We can't handle that much suffering.

MOVING TOWARD PEACE

At the Clinton Global Initiative inaugural conference that I was invited to, Bill Clinton said, "If we just stop and think, the world would be a better place." And so, I ask you to stop and think. How can we move from a culture of war to a culture of peace? How can we stop this craziness? Is it even possible? Despite the guns, and bombs, and wars that surround us, many of the experts whom I interviewed point to situations in which it is very possible, places where peace—not conflict—have reigned. For instance, weapons expert Joe Cirincione told me, "When you talk about peace or ending conflict, people ask, 'Well, how can you do that? That's Utopian.' But I say look at Europe. It is unthinkable that Germany and France would go to war with each other now. But that is exactly what they used to do every generation from before there was a Germany and France, when it was just Franks and Goths. They don't do that anymore. Europe has been at peace for its longest period in history. This was the most violent continent on earth, and it isn't anymore. And if we can do that in Europe, we can do it anywhere."

In addition to all of his other endeavors, Ted Turner has founded the United Nations Foundation, a non-governmental organization that works full-time alongside the UN and individual governments to rid the world of weapons of mass destruction. He wouldn't be involved in this kind of work unless he believed that peace is possible. "Peace is a state of existence," Ted told me, "and we certainly can get there. We just have to commit ourselves. All we have to do is look at the example that Costa Rica set. They've had no bombings for sixty years. Instead of wasting their resources on military weapons, they spend it on education, healthcare, and technology."

Mark Gerzon, in crafting the mission for his Mediators Foundation, had spoken to me about the beauty of Nelson Mandela's work in South Africa. Mandela held out a vision that all-out war in his country would be disastrous. Disastrous for blacks and disastrous for whites. Peace wasn't achieved in South Africa just because everyone suddenly loved one another. But blacks and whites looked straight into the barrel of a gun and decided that the benefits of peace, and ending Apartheid, were going to be greater than the benefits of going to war over Apartheid." And that's the key shift in perception: when it becomes clear to everyone that the benefits of peace outweigh the benefits of war.

THE TRAUMA VORTEX

Why are we so crazy? Why are we so crazy? Why do we think we are going to win wars against the so-called terror? We will never win a war against terror as long as there are conditions in the world that make people desperate.

—ARCHBISHOP DESMOND TUTU

My sister Liz and her husband, Jim, live in downtown Manhattan. On September 11, 2001, it was her turn to take their two-year-old daughter, Aidan, to the Buckle My Shoe Preschool, three blocks from the World Trade Center. They usually alternated the drop-off, and when it was Liz's turn, afterwards, she would normally walk to the World Trade Center subway station to pick up the train that would take her to her graphic design business, where she would start her workday.

"It was my turn to stay home that day," Jim told me, "and I wasn't hurrying to work. I decided to put dinner in a crock-pot so we wouldn't have to cook when we got home at night." He turned on the morning news while he prepared the meal and saw that the first World Trade Center tower had been hit. "It didn't change anything. I kept right on cooking," he explained. "A horrible accident, I thought. I plugged in the pot and walked outside. The towers are right there—about twenty blocks away; you can see them from our place."

Like most of us, he believed that a commuter plane had hit the building. He wondered how firemen would put out this fire. Since Liz had just left with their two-year-old, he wondered whether she was close by. He started weighing his options when he realized that she might return with Aidan. "This was a little frightening for me, because now I had to decide whether I should try to find them or wait for them at home," Jim told me. "There are so many different ways to get there, so I decided the best thing to do was just hang out. 'She sees the accident,' I told myself. 'She knows. She'll probably come back.'

"Suddenly there was so much activity downtown, fire engines, sirens, the hole in the building," Jim continued, "papers were blowing up our street like confetti in some sort of parade. It was the craziest thing. All the neighbors were standing outside. In that moment, I didn't believe there was any real danger for my family; everything was fine with us. I talked with my neighbors about how the fire department was going to rescue the people who were on the floors above the fire. We speculated about how many people got hurt. And as we were standing there looking up, we watched the other plane come around. It hit the second building so hard I could feel the heat from the explosion.

"The street fell silent. All the people were outside, it was dead quiet, and nobody knew how to act until someone answered a ringing cell phone and said, 'We're being attacked.' That's when I got afraid. I had to get my wife and my daughter. Not only that—but Liz was about to enter the basement of the World Trade Center. That's her subway stop. My daughter's daycare was in an old bank building that had glass walls ceiling to floor. I was in a panic."

Soon police and fire engines and ambulances were everywhere. It was a crazy warzone, but twenty minutes after it all began Jim said to himself, "I don't care; I've got to find them somehow. I walked up to 6th Avenue—Liz's favorite route— and as I was looking up, I saw the flames and people jumping out of the towers. You hear about a few people jumping, but it was raining people. It was horrifying. And then I noticed the top of one building tilt a bit, and it just came down."

A big waft of smoke and dust started coming his way. Everyone turned to run from it, but Jim ran into it. "A cop grabbed me by my arm and said, 'Stop! You can't go down there!'"

"But my wife and daughter are there," Jim cried.

The policeman had compassion and let him pass. Cars were turning around mid-street and people were running and the air was thick with smoke and debris, but Jim ran into it. He ran all the way to the daycare center and when he got there he saw that the teachers had gathered all sixty kids into a back room. He breathed a huge sigh of relief as he saw his daughter, Aidan, in the corner. All the children were singing songs, oblivious to what was going on. He learned that Liz had left before the first plane hit. He offered their nearby apartment as a sanctuary to any parents who wanted to leave the school.

Everything was white with dust, including Jim. He put his daughter in her stroller and along with another parent, Sheryl, and her son, and made preparations to leave. "When we got to the door, Sheryl said, 'Maybe we should cover their faces, it's really dusty out there.' I went into the men's room to get some towels when the second tower started falling. It was an earth-quake. Somebody screamed, 'We're being bombed!' We had no idea what was going on outside. The building shook and the lights went out. Things fell off the shelves and again all of this smoke. One of the teachers ran up, grabbed our kids and pulled them back into the room in case the windows broke. We all hud-dled in the room again. At that point, the phone rang which was just unbelievable because the phones were all down. It was Liz. Somebody said, 'She's okay, she's fine.' When the dust settled, Sheryl and I grabbed our kids, covered their faces, left the stroll-ers, and we just ran out of there all the way home."

Jim was in a state of disbelief. "I was a forty-five-year-old man, and I couldn't wrap my brain around the fact that we were under attack. I've never known anything like that. One of the most profound moments was turning around as I was running and seeing both towers gone. It was pretty devastating. How could anyone survive that? They're huge buildings. And then I thought: How is this going to change everything?"

Great question. Because the events of that day did, indeed, change everything for the people of New York, our nation, and the world.

TRAPPED IN THE TRAUMA VORTEX

A few short months after the fall of the Twin Towers and the attack on the Pentagon, President George W. Bush decided to play G.I. Joe with the media and the American people. The Bush Doctrine advocated preemptive strikes—the rules of government had changed. And so he dragged the US and our military industrial complex into nearly a decade of senseless war in Iraq that drained our economy, sacrificed our youth, and squandered the empathy the world felt for our suffering in the aftermath of the attack. (Even crowds in Tehran had held candlelight vigils immediately after 9/11 in honor of the fallen.)

That war also damaged our national standing and credibility. The fact that Iraq had nothing to do with the attacks on 9/11 was clear to the majority of people, but seemingly irrelevant to our leaders. And what was worse, the media believing its own truth kept pumping this information into the hearts and minds of the American psyche. We all now know those fearsome "Weapons of Mass Destruction" tales were a hoax. Our government desperately needed an enemy—someone against whom it could vent its rage; someone from whom it could exact revenge. Al Qaeda was too amorphous; Osama Bin Laden still too elusive and purportedly hiding out in his Afghani caves. So we found our target in Saddam Hussein. And we struck with "shock and awe."

This is how President George W. Bush had pulled us into the essence of the trauma vortex. What is the trauma vortex? Its simple. Think of a whirlpool in which an act of violence perpetrated against innocent people breeds trauma, which then breeds rage and retaliation on the part of the victims, which then breeds trauma on the other side, which then breeds their rage and retaliation, and on and on… in an endlessly descending spiral of hatred and dehumanization, retribution, and mutual destruction.

Los Angeles trauma expert and psychotherapist Gina Ross explains its wider implications. "Unhealed trauma is not static," she told me. "It keeps augmenting, it keeps amplifying. And so, from something that just made a small part of your life dysfunctional, it can spread to a bigger and bigger part of your life, and then the lives of the people around you, and then your community. The metaphor of the trauma vortex (as coined by Dr. Peter Levine) is expressive of its dynamic nature—this impulsive energy that keeps growing and creating a life of its own. It is like a virus of pain and suffering and dysfunction." The never-ending struggles in Rwanda, Ireland, Gaza, the Congo, and Zimbabwe, the wars in Iraq and Afghanistan, the destruction of Libya and Syria, and the rise of ISIS—all spawned by Al Qaeda's initial attack on the United States. And on it goes. Heartbreaking examples of this virus that holds people and communities hostage and prevents them from growing as modern civilized societies.

I had an opportunity to attend the Dalai Lama Peace Summit, where I met with Nobel Peace Laureate Mairead Maguire. To start, she spoke about compassion. The word "compassion" comes from the Latin words "cum" and "patta," which mean to suffer with. It's a very interesting concept, because we all know life is suffering. Everybody suffers. There can be great joy, if we are prepared to walk in solidarity with people who are suffering. Mairead told me that the World Health Organization considers violence a preventable disease. "We were not born violent," she said. "Our culture teaches us to become violent." And what's worse, it's holding back the progress of the human spirit.

She continued, "I think the most important thing is to absolutely believe that peace is possible, and for everyone to be convinced that violence is not going to get us there. Violence, no matter where it comes from, just creates more violence and forms a vicious circle. For the vast majority of people in Northern Ireland, we were caught in a circle of violence. One day there was a bomb from the IRA and the next it was the loyalist paramilitaries, or the British Army and police. It seemed to be an ever-increasing circle of violence. There seemed no way to stop it. Tragically, when children were killed, it touched the hearts of many people. The children were only six weeks old, three years old, and eight years old. To see a young family just wiped out like that was the breaking point."

When the world saw what happened, people decided this violence has got to stop, and began to organize for peace. It was the beginning of the Peace People Rallies. More than half a million people marched in Northern Ireland, Southern Ireland, and England. People wanted peace. There was a 70 percent decrease in the rate of violence, and twenty-five years later the conflict finally ended. It took a change in perception, but once faced with the horror, people chose peace. It started with a call to deal with the root causes of the violence, and people began to do that. And it wasn't easy.

According to Maguire, "Politicians said, 'You can't have people from the paramilitary group speaking.' But if you don't speak to your enemies, how are you going to solve the problem? We tried to stop the demonization of people in our society and start the serious dialog. That helped the process, and then we created platforms for all different political parties to speak about the conflict … to find common ground."

Look at the root causes of violence here in the United States. It's almost always a call for basic civil rights. Why in the mid-sixties did the Civil Rights Movement come onto the streets? To ask for basic civil liberties.

"Trauma is a common reality," says Gina Ross. It is a daily reality. It happens every day. Traumatic events happen every single day. It is very unlikely that somebody is going to live a lifetime without encountering traumatic events in their lives. So, what do we do with this amount of trauma in the world? We compassionately learn to use it as a starting point in a conversation about peace. And until we start doing that, we will all continue to be trapped in the cycle of violence.

I certainly learned that one day as I passed through JFK International Airport on my way out west. I hadn't flown for a while, and I had a confrontation at the airport with TSA agents when I was asked to take off my shoes, belt, and other accessories and to leave behind my toothpaste and a bottle of water. I was threatened with arrest when I protested their order to turn over my water bottle. For Christ's sake! What did a TSA agent need to confiscate that was hidden in my water bottle? The whole idea seemed ludicrous at the time. We were heading down a path of fear. And why? What were we fighting for?

At this critical juncture, I realized we have all become hostages in our own country. We were now all "imprisoned" for the sake of our own safety, just like I had been in Israel during the first Gulf War. As I flew to Aspen, Colorado, I kept thinking about the famous line from Franklin Delano Roosevelt's first Inaugural Address: "The only thing we have to fear is fear itself." Fear had created this state of affairs, and again, I felt claustrophobic, as if I were choking.

While I was in Aspen attending Aspen's Renewable Energy Day, I met environmentalist Doug Cohen. He asked if I was planning to attend the United Nations International Day of Peace. I was confused. International Day of Peace? I was perplexed. Even as I made my way to the UN event, I didn't understand. What were Jane Goodall, Elie Wiesel, Yoko Ono, and Michael Douglas doing at the United Nations? For peace? As the ceremony began, I watched as many children entered the ceremony holding the flags of the world. They all looked so innocent, happy, and calm. The Secretary General Ban Ki Moon gave his inaugural address, introducing the Peace Ambassadors, and talking about the urgency of nuclear disarmament and the need to remove these devices. What was striking was the moment that all the Peace Ambassadors stood around the Peace Bell on the stage with him. The Peace Bell had Japanese writing on it. As he finished his address with the ringing of the bell, it all became clear to me. The

Hiroshima bell was the common thread from which all humanity can learn. To see front and center the eye of hate and evil that twisted the world into devastation and turmoil.

Author and philosopher Matthew Fox, whose latest book is titled *Recovering the Sacred Masculine: The Hidden Spirituality of Men* has spent quite a bit of time talking to me about the role of our primordial biology in perpetuating war and reprisal. He explained that we go to war when we're working out of our reptilian brains. "We've all got this 420-million-year-old reptilian brain in us," he said, "and it's win or lose with a crocodile, in case you haven't noticed. The way men prove their identity, their masculinity is to win over someone else, to be number one, to make war, to eat your enemy—which is literally what a lot of our ancestors did in cannibal and hunter-gatherer times. Well, that energy is obviously war energy."

Fear activates the brain, putting us into a reptilian state of self-preservation. Fear breeds more violence, and then retaliation in an endless cycle. But as Matthew Fox explains, fear in and of itself is very useful. "It prevents us from walking across a busy street at the wrong time and in the wrong places. So fear isn't so negative in itself, but as St. Thomas Aquinas told us in the thirteenth century, fear is such a powerful emotion in humans that it can take over the heart and drive out all compassion. So, this is why fear is the opposite of love—it drives out love. Ultimately, we cannot choose to live both a life of fear and a life of love; it's one or the other. And it's clear that since 9/11 a lot of our political discourse has been whipping up hysteria around fear."

We are now living in a perpetual culture of war and find ourselves stripped of our freedoms—hostages in our own nation. I am disturbed about the quality of our lives and how people behave even in daily situations. What are we vibrating? Positive or negative energy? Light or dark? Love or fear? And why? What has caused this? How did we get here?

As Fox asserts, fear activates our primitive, reptilian state of self-preservation. If we are caught in the trauma vortex—in which trauma begets fear, and fear begets violence, and violence begets retaliation, and retaliation begets more trauma, in an endless cycle—there is no possibility of reconciliation, and we face continual conflict. Indeed, the human psyche is conditioned to react as if everyone is out to kill us. But if we live in that worldview, we have no peace. We are already dead inside. Numb. Angry. Vengeful. Hurting. Closed off to the beauty and preciousness of life. So what are we so afraid of?

Gerzon says that what is behind our current world conflicts is not necessarily what we think it is. "Ironically, I see more violence committed on behalf of identities than on behalf of food and land," explains Gerzon. "People will risk their lives sooner than they'll risk their identities. That's how precious our identities are to us. If it were only food, water, and shelter, a lot of conflicts could be resolved. But it's food, water, shelter, and *identity*. However, identity alone is not the problem. It's our attachment to our identities."

Gerzon went on to explain that if you removed the Jewishness, or Christianness, or Muslimness from some Jews, Christians, and Muslims, "they'd be immobilized. They'd be paralyzed. They'd be in shock. They'd be in crisis." It's the strong adherence to these identities that cause us to build fences around ourselves—keeping the other out, and preventing us from finding common ground and unity which would bring resolution to our differences.

I was fortunate enough to attend the UN General Assembly Millennium Award show where Archbishop Desmond Tutu was receiving a lifetime achievement award, and I recorded the final words of Tutu's speech. To combat our sense of isolation, our intense adherence to identities, our reaction to fear and trauma, Tutu stressed the clear interdependence of mankind, the weaving together of our fates and our lives, our oneness:

"You can't be human all on your own. You need two people to come together before you could even be an idea. I wouldn't know how to think as a human being. I wouldn't know how to speak as a human being. I wouldn't know how to walk as a human being. I wouldn't know how to be human, except by learning from other human beings. We are made for interdependence. We are made for family. If we are family, how can we still tolerate spending billions or maybe trillions on instruments of death and destruction when a minute little fraction of those budgets would ensure that children everywhere would have clean water to drink and enough food to eat? They would have a decent home, would have good education, would have affordable healthcare. Why are we so crazy? Why are we so crazy? Why do we think we are going to win wars against the so-called terror? We will never win a war against terror as long as there are conditions in the world that make people desperate.

"We are family. We are family. In our home, in this planet, we are family—sisters and brothers who can survive only together. We can be humans only together. We can be safe only together. We can be prosperous only together, together, together, together."

MILITATING FOR PEACE

If you want to change the world, start with yourself. Be a good example. Otherwise you'll end up being an angry peace activist, which is a contradiction.

—DEEPAK CHOPRA

It began at the University of Massachusetts at Amherst in 1993. Sifting through my scrapbook, I noticed my original Giving Tree pamphlet, which I had produced thirty years ago. I had this lofty idea I was going to save the world by planting trees. What was I thinking? Back then I was committed to the idea that if all I could do was just one thing to save the world, I would plant trees. That's where I would take my stand. Along with my scrapbook, I came across a VHS copy of the commencement address from author John Updike. I brushed off the dust, placed it into the VHS machine, and hit play.

"My thought for you this morning is that you may not be much different. You too are graduating into times when history is more like a short story collection than a novel. You are concerned about finding your niche in the economy, as were we. You are looking into family life as the vehicle of happiness, as did we, and perhaps you distrust generalizations, as did we. I distrust even the ones I am now making. History tints us like fish that swim through colored water, but our bones are all fish bones.

"The human species, with its internal drives and conflicts, is a constant; a Cro-Magnon man of thirty-five thousand years ago dressed in academic garb and placed on this platform, would not look out of place. We are born into history, and graduate into it, but our animal optimism, and our cerebral capacity to plan our own personal futures, exists independently of history. The individual is the unit of measure. Nowhere is this truer than in the United States."

Updike continued, "I said that I was conditioned to believe that America has a heart of gold. Mine may be the last generation that could believe this easily. But international events in the four years since you've entered the university make it easier it seems to me—a newly exciting time to be American. We are no longer obliged to pour our strength into a cold war of reaction and counter blow; we have moved from a dualistic to a pluralistic world, a world in which our national gifts are by no means obsolete. What are those national gifts? At a stab, they are: good humor, optimism, the ability to improvise, the willingness to learn, and the respect for the individual. You graduating seniors are the latest embodiments of these qualities. The newest addition. Thanks to television, computers, and an openness that came with the sixties, you are savvy in ways in which my generation was not. What you know about the facts of life, and what you understand of tolerance and acceptance, and the multiform ways of being human, puts 1954 to shame. But your generational savviness, one that could only be in our age of imagery and sound bites, is a matter more of imagery than of the heft of real things; of earth and the tools that bit by bit move it. You cannot but learn more of the worlds heft as you take it now into your hands. Take it up—reverently—for it is an old piece of clay with millions of thumbprints on it."

As I hit the pause button, I thought about the importance of bringing this truth forward. Perhaps this crazy idea I had thirty years ago about planting trees to achieve peace may have some merit. After the tape ended, I switched back and forth from Fox News to CNN. Clearly, I needed some inspiration, hope, or some way to reactivate my activism.

It wasn't long before I received a call from Jodie Evans, founder of CODEPINK, a woman's peace activist group, asking me to come backstage at the Greek Theatre to join the ranks of Carlos Santana and Danny Glover for an evening of activism and, of course, peace awareness. I was asked to dress in pink. Upon arrival, I walked over to the CODEPINK booth and asked to hand out peace stickers saying "Make Love Not War" to everyone entering the Greek Theatre. When the concert started, we were asked to join the other peace activists backstage, and it started to look like less of a concert and more of a rally. Different activists, one by one, paraded on stage every twenty minutes, ranting about social issues ranging from the environment to food sources, human justice to social justice, and even sex trafficking. It seemed like every social issue was also a peace issue. I even had a chance to meet one of the founders of the woman's movement, Dolores Huerta.

Backstage, I spent more time with Jodie. She seemed joyously happy about how the event was rolling out, though underneath there was a deep sense of frustration on her face. As the night progressed, she felt compelled to talk and share her frog story.

"You know the story about the frog? The frog that you put in water, and how you just turn the heat up a little at a time. If you threw him in hot water, he would jump out, but if the water gets hotter and hotter a little at a time, the frog passively stays and eventually fries to death. We're kind of like that. The media is just frying everybody's brain slowly. This media entity wants to protect itself, and if it were to tell the truth about what we're doing out in the world, people will quit behaving, or there'll be riots in the streets." She continued, "I mean, do we ever sit and think about the cost of war? Nobody wins in war. It's devastating."

When the night concluded, I thanked Jodie and her fellow pink peace activists. I felt devirginized to the movement, part of a collective, part of a greater whole, though I wasn't entirely sure what my role would be in this peace movement. I wasn't even sure if there was any merit in being a peace activist in the twenty-first century. I had lots of questions. I was pivoting into this peace movement, which seemed like a bicycle wheel. At its core was the desire for peace, but the movement had lots of spokes.

As fate would have it, I had met the ninety-one-year-old legendary folk singer and peace activist Pete Seeger at the UN during an International Day of Peace celebration, where he was invited to ring the Peace Bell. After the equinox ceremony, I was invited by my friend Phil Sauers to come and meet Seeger in his hometown in Beacon, New York to talk further. When I arrived at his small suburb outside town, I found him standing with other activists on a street corner waving peace signs. My memories of Pete Seeger from when I was a kid run the gauntlet from radical fascist groups claiming he was a communist to my Uncle John sharing stories of him marching with Seeger and Martin Luther King, Jr., to hearing his song "If I Had a Hammer" at summer camp. When I arrived, I was informed by the peaceniks that for the past six years Pete Seeger and his fellow peace comrades congregated at this small street corner every Sunday as part of a vigil to show solidarity and protest against the war. As I continued talking to Pete and the other peace activists, I couldn't help but notice the traffic of cars and oddly how each of them continued to honk their horns. Across the street stood roughly ten war veterans holding their own demonstration. This time, conversely, the opposite held up signs of pro-war, pro-Navy, pro-US, and pro-Army. All in the name of supporting our troops.

As people drove through the Beacon intersection honking, I kept asking myself, are they honking for war or for peace? Are they aware of the distinction between being pro-war versus pro-peace? Even the peaceniks seemed puzzled in terms of who they were choosing. Were they agreeing with "War is Strength" or "Live Free or Die" or "God Bless America" or are they as just as confused as I am?

In our conversations, Pete seemed to be inspired by the fantastic Baptist preacher Martin Luther King, Jr., who he praised for his nonviolence approach.

I asked him if he or his fellow peaceniks had tried to converse with the veterans across the street. He simply smiled. I thought co-existing wasn't enough, so I took it upon myself to cross the street and to engage the local uber-patriotic veterans and was pleasantly greeted with "Go f*** yourself" when I asked about one of their signs saying, "Pete Seeger is a Communist Stooge." I became aware that none of the veterans really wanted to talk. They seemed genuinely interested in just showing their pro-war signs, and as a war veteran wielding an American flag said, "Our guys are over there fighting; we've got to support the troops." One of the pro-troops protesters, a Navy Seal, kept trying to persuade them from conversing with me at all, until finally it was obvious that I wasn't leaving until I spoke with one of them. Finally, an enraged protester said to me, "Those guys over there think they are going to bring peace and prosperity to the world by blowing bubbles and doing dances. Wars have been going on for ten thousand years. This is nothing new."

As I returned back to the peaceniks, I realized this was a great example of how divided our country is and how we live completely unaware of the two sides of the war versus peace issue, but the issue continues to be unresolved. I huddled back with the peaceniks as we all joined in a circle with Pete and his banjo. We ended up singing for another twenty minutes, with lots of hugs and handshaking goodbyes. As the day concluded, I was dropped off at the Beacon train station.

During that train ride, I kept thinking, "Why is peace so difficult to achieve?" Are we numbed by our pop culture to think that war doesn't traumatize us? Are these polarized forces pushing our world backward or forward? I decided to visit one of my favorite places in Fresh Meadows Corona Park, the symbolic unisphere. I was informed that when the structure was constructed during the World's Fair, back in 1964, it was a time of change—a year that called upon man to face new challenges, and to shape the world we dreamed about. Supposedly, the architects even created a street in the park called Peace Avenue. I was super confused on the meaning of peace. Do you have to be an activist in order to be peaceful? Is there really any relevance between peace and my tree planting? When I arrived at the park, I grabbed a map to locate Peace Avenue. It took about thirty minutes for me to navigate the area in the park. There was no longer any street sign for Peace Avenue, just a field of grass. The city never created a permanent street sign at the location. Perhaps the existence of a street sign was unimportant in the scheme of things. I was dumfounded. I was looking for a sign, literally looking for a sign, that didn't exist.

I found a place to sit and reflect about my journey and the subversive culture of war embedded in comic games and video games. I thought about my time in Japan visiting Hiroshima, and now in my own backyard of the World Trade Center, and the 9/11 memorial. This cycle of violence seemed endless. Are we all just part of one human trauma vortex? Is this an insane existence?

As I was leaving Corona Park, I received a call from the organizers of Universal Peace Day inviting me to plant a tree at the Church of St. Paul and St. Andrew in Manhattan. Maybe peace is not that hard. Maybe peace is as simple as putting a tree in the ground. One act by one person. I thought about my roots, and my time back at UMASS Amherst, and of my first tree planting venture. I responded positively and agreed to the peace tree planting. I was informed the planting would commemorate the bombing of Nagasaki. The event seemed right up my alley, so I invited my brother-in-law Jim and my nephew Gabriel to join. I was astutely surprised on the low turnout of people, but I kept my spirits up as I wanted my nephew to appreciate the endeavor. While at the church, I was pleasantly surprised that when we asked my nephew the meaning of peace, it took him only a few moments to respond by saying, "When wars stop."

The ceremony began with a little ukulele ceremonial song with about fifteen people gathered in a circle. I grabbed the shovel and began to hit the surface where I was planning to root this tree. I was unpleasantly shocked as the soil was layered underneath with about two feet of concrete. How's my tree going to take root? Politely, I found my way to the minister to chat about what I had discovered, only to find out there was no alternative planting ground. Rather than ruin the event for my nephew, we went through the motions of the tree planting, though the whole experience felt awkward and inauthentic.

As I realized that this peace tree would not take root, I thought perhaps there was something for me to learn here. I was frustrated, angry, and resigned. What was supposed to be a simple act of kindness had turned into a nightmare—a fake exercise. Why?

A PEACE MARCH UNNOTICED

What do we want? Peace. When do we want it? Now! What do we want? Peace! When do we want it? Now! I was standing in the middle of the rain with a peace parrot on my shoulder as students were chanting. It was the annual World Peace March during which the Hiroshima Torch visits more than 160 countries over a ninety-day period. This particular world march began in New Zealand on October 2, 2009, the anniversary of Gandhi's birth—declared by the United Nations as the "International Day of Non-Violence"—and concluded in Argentina on January 2, 2010. In the United States, the march began in Borough Hall in downtown Brooklyn. About three hundred activists had gathered that morning and proceeded en masse across the Brooklyn Bridge. Despite the heavy rains, I remember being told that the press covering the event would formally greet us when we reached City Hall in Manhattan. But nobody came. Not even the mayor. No one. The march wasn't mentioned in any of the New York publications or on the local news. By contrast, in Europe and the rest of the world hundreds of articles were published, and the march was well received by all the local news agencies. The lack of response made me wonder what it would take for America to wake up.

I know in my heart peace protests are important as they make everyone stop and take notice of important issues. But I was unable to find coherence. The peace I was seeking was much deeper, and it dawned on me that I was coming at it from the wrong direction. Perhaps I needed to look within myself. I sought counsel from Deepak Chopra. He told me, "If you want to change the world, start with yourself. Be a good example. Otherwise you'll end up being an angry peace activist, which is a contradiction." There it was again: the world is as you are.

THE BEACH BOYS
AND THE MAHARISHI

If the forest is to be green, every tree must be green. If there's going to be peace on Earth, then everyone has to feel that quality of peace.

—MAHARISHI MAHESH YOGI

It was spring. I was living down by the beach in Marina del Rey. I noticed my personal and business life were all intertwined with my quest for peace. I really didn't know what to do. I had hit a wall, and worse, my film funds were diminishing. I had spent twenty-four months filming my documentary meant to change the world, and I was even more perplexed on the meaning of peace than when I had started. I needed to act. I felt the need to do something quickly. I reached out to an old marketing friend, Del Breckenfeld, who works at Fender Musical Instruments. I recalled him donating guitars for charitable functions and thought perhaps a peace/tree fundraiser with a musical performance would be the solution for my current malaise. I asked for a public relations recommendation, and he politely suggested Putnam & Smith.

We all convened down in Sherman Oaks for a typical Hollywood luncheon. I met publicist Cherry Smith and her assistant Britta. We discussed her firm producing a fundraiser for my peace tree film. The conversation ran smoothly for roughly an hour but throughout the lunch I kept finding myself staring at her assistant Britta's beautiful blue eyes. After lunch concluded, I decided to venture forward with the fundraiser. I waited a few days after our initial meeting to catch up with Britta, see how our event was progressing, and what was needed from our entertainment firm. To be honest, I couldn't stop thinking about her and the moments we had locked eyes during the meeting. We talked a bit on the phone about the event, and then I gained the courage to ask her out. Apparently, I surprised her. It took her a few seconds to gain her composure, but she politely responded and said yes.

That evening we met up at the Cheesecake Factory. I found out that Britta grew up in a small town in Iowa. At first, she seemed overly quiet, though sweet and friendly. I was still mesmerized by her blue eyes. After conversing with her for about an hour, I was slowly falling in love. Within the next few hours, we talked about everything: life, purpose, past relationships. I realized we had a lot in common. We talked for a few more

hours, and after dinner we proceeded to the AMC theatre to
see the animated feature film *Up*. As the night progressed, I
sensed an inner feeling inside, something I hadn't felt in a long
time. As the date concluded, I walked her to her car. I was hesitant about kissing her. I wanted to leave a good first impression.
As I slowly moved in to kiss her on the cheek, she moved her
face to join my lips. As our lips collapsed together, a wonderful
feeling inside overtook my whole body.

Perhaps that kiss was the beginning of a new chapter in my
life. Britta and I ended up spending that entire summer together. It was a magical summer filled with love, wine, and roman-
tic evenings down by the beach. Our relationship was growing
quickly. I was falling in love with a small-town girl from Iowa.
On one hand, my heart had found peace by falling for Britta,
but on the other hand, I was becoming even more frustrated
in solving the quintessential meaning of world peace. Britta seemed intrigued about my peace journey and film career.
She was compassionate about helping me along my journey. She
had come with me to the Pete Seeger corner rally to observe
first hand the opposition. When I returned from the Brooklyn
World march, she could sense my frustration. I think she was
just as confused as I was about the journey I was taking, but she
never gave up hope that I would find answers to the questions
that were driving me. I kept thinking to myself, "Why does a
Midwest girl want to be dating a New York Yankee? Would love
be my answer to peace?"

I kept reminding myself of Deepak Chopra opening my
eyes to the idea of meditation, consciousness, and the lessons

from his friend Maharishi Mahesh Yogi. I went online and started plugging in those words on the Google search bar. Peace.
Inner peace. Meditation. Maharishi. What was Deepak trying
to tell me? You can't be an angry peace activist to be a peace-
maker. What an oxymoron. Who was this character Maharishi
Mahesh Yogi? In my investigation, I discovered that Maharishi
had his own University in Fairfield, Iowa, and surprisingly the
Beach Boys were planning to perform Labor Day weekend
there. I didn't know who this Maharishi character was, or why
he would have his own university, but I thought maybe God
was telling me something. I figured my girlfriend from Iowa
and I could use a break, so off we went. Besides, who doesn't
love the Beach Boys?

It was our first getaway weekend. Upon arriving, we met up
with the local publicist of the University, Ken Chawkin, who
gave us a tour. There was a lot of talk about Transcendental
Meditation, but I wasn't sure what it had to do with me. After
the Beach Boys concert, Britta and I had a chance to go backstage and meet Mike Love, a co-founder and lyricist for the
band. In addition to singing and songwriting, I found out Mike
was a Transcendental Meditation (TM) teacher. I was curious
to learn what the connection was between a rock and roll musician and Transcendental Meditation, so we sat down to talk
about the meaning of life.

"We'd been on our Surfing Safari," he started. "We'd done
Good Vibrations and the Pet Sounds album, and had all these
great experiences. This is a whole different realm that I ventured into. It's kind of like you're on a spiritual safari." He had

met the Maharishi in Paris in 1967 at the UNICEF Christmas benefit event where Maharishi spoke on world peace. After the concert, Mike met up with Maharishi, where he was initiated by Maharishi himself. "The first time I meditated with Maharishi it was so easy to do. Anyone could do it. We were so peaceful. I've never felt so peaceful all my life."

I could sense from talking with Mike that Maharishi had a tremendous impact on his life. I asked Mike if he could share some of the wisdom that Maharishi shared with him in Paris. Quoting the Maharishi, Mike said, "Modern psychology says man has been using only a small portion of the mind. Transcendental Meditation is a way to enable every man to make use of his full mental potential. Imagine the development in all fields of civilization when every man will be using his full mental potential. If the forest is to be green, every tree must be green. If there's going to be peace on Earth, then everyone has to feel that quality of peace." I'd always thought of peace and the sixties as hippies smoking marijuana and wearing tie dyes. What did the forest have to do with it? And how was this concept connected to my original idea of planting trees? Had I been on to something all along?

Mike mentioned a getaway in Rishikesh, India, with Maharishi, the Beatles, and Donovan back in the day. What had they found in India? I had to know. Later, when I had a chance to visit with the legendary folk singer Donovan, hoping he could shed some light on what drew them to India, he laughed when I asked him. "What led me to study with the Maharishi Mahesh Yogi?"

He smiled, "As my songs say, before I met Maharishi, I was searching and studying the teachings. George Harrison was studying too and he and I would hang out and swap books. I'd give him the *Diamond Sutra*, the Buddhist classic, and he gave me *The Autobiography of a Yogi* by Yogananda. We both spoke of how we really needed a true yogi to teach us the pure form of meditation. At the time George was studying sitar in India with Ravi Shankar. Patti Boyd (George's wife) attended a Maharishi lecture in a Himalayan cave with Shankar's female relatives. When George and Patti had returned to England, Patti saw on television that the Maharishi was in England and invited the Beatles to come out. And then one day, George said, 'He's here. This is the guy. He's got everything we need.' I then met up with the Maharishi in Los Angeles and was initiated by him. It was like falling slowly down the rabbit hole like in *Alice in Wonderland*."

I was fascinated as Donovan recounted his journey. I was curious to know what they were searching for with meditation. Donovan again smiled warmly saying, "This reads like a science fiction story at first, but listen to this. The ancient book *The Upanishads* best describes the purpose of true meditation. It says the human being lives on three levels of consciousness: waking, sleeping, and dreamless sleep. There is a fourth level, which is called super conscious transcendental vision. Entering this fourth level is achieved through true meditation. This is your true home. The unified field and the effect is you now have an understanding of the unity of all things, and you are all things. This is what all the teachings intellectually describe in the books, and now we could experience it ourselves.

"If everyone feels unified, why would you want to kill your brother and sister on the planet? Why would you want to poison the river? Why would you want to annihilate the whole planet with a nuclear warhead? If you felt unified you would be killing yourself. This teaching had been lost through the last two-thousand years in the West. That was the reason why we were searching; to see if there really was a fourth level of consciousness. We'd been plunging in with sacred plants, with mescaline, pot, and LSD, but it was too traumatic and temporary. Maharishi taught us how we dive deep down effortlessly with Transcendental Meditation into our fourth level of consciousness."

I could see in Donovan's eyes, as he was sharing, his story of divine inspiration. He picked up his guitar and started to play for me. He mentioned his guitar had an Irish name, Kelly. I could sense as he started to play his mind was traveling back in time to that special place. "People ask me, what were the sixties all about? Why do they reverberate 'til today? It can be described as a renaissance period, which included freedom of speech, civil rights, protest, ecology, philosophy, meditation, women's rights, and unity consciousness. All being explored in the twentieth century. My own feeling is that the sixties were the cry. The cry was very loud. Millions of people were born after the Second World War. It was a generation that grew up after war, who never wanted a war again. The sixties were a direct cry for sanity in a world that was bent on destroying itself."

He continued to strum his guitar and began to sing "The Hurdy-Gurdy Man" with a verse that was never recorded before. "When truth gets buried deep beneath a thousand years asleep, time demands a turn-around, and once again the truth is found." He smiled, "That one was written with George in Rishikesh." Donovan continued, almost in a whisper, "George Harrison gave me the tambura that he brought from India. I went straight into the studio and produced the sound called 'The Hurdy-Gurdy Man,' which in fact is like a pagan Celtic rock track, the sound we now call British classic rock."

"The Hurdy-Gurdy Man" is a very well-known song, but the original hurdy-gurdy man played the instrument two hundred years ago called the hurdy-gurdy. In those times, news was passed on in songs through folk music. Hurdy-gurdies produce sound by a hand crank-turned, rosined wheel rubbing against bowed strings and gives off a sound that resonates, like bagpipes. The hurdy-gurdy man would place it around his neck as he traveled from town to town singing out the news.

Donovan continued, "So all over the world, there were these traveling musicians. That's it. The Hurdy-Gurdy Man brings the news and here comes the news. In our fourth level of consciousness, the Hurdy-Gurdy Man is Maharishi. And the Hurdy-Gurdy man is me. The Hurdy-Gurdy men are the Beatles, and all the conscious poets and music makers. Anyone who then forms their song with this extraordinary powerful wisdom that was rediscovered in the sixties by many, not just us, brings forth that truth. When I came out of India, I brought the technique to my millions of fans." Donovan added, "Maharishi's simple Transcendental Meditation is the key to the fourth level, the unified field. We need to save the planet, so the more people that mediate the better. The Maharishi encourages to teach it in school, and that's now happening. The David Lynch Foundation and I began The Donovan Children's Fund to do just that."

As Donovan finished playing the Hurdy-Gurdy song, I felt a huge sense of relief overcome him as he was sharing this information with me. I could sense the importance of him sharing about his guru, and the importance of this moment of him passing his wisdom teachings onto me for my film. And he wasn't finished. He requested of me to meet the legendary filmmaker David Lynch. He thought it would be helpful in my transformative journey and planned on making an introduction.

I politely said yes, as who wouldn't want to meet the acclaimed director. Though I have to admit, I was even more confused as to why he wanted me to meet David Lynch. I didn't know then that Lynch was devoted to making sure every person and child everywhere who wants to learn to meditate has the means to do so. "Doesn't he direct dark movies like *Mulholland Drive*, *Blue Velvet*, *Eraserhead*, and *Lost Highway*?" I thought. Not exactly the lightness of being I was looking for, but Donovan said, "You will be surprised with David. Awakened artists can of course create work to show the suffering of humanity, and in doing so, awaken our compassion." I still had my reservations about David but regardless, I complied and said yes, I would love to meet the great David Lynch. Donovan and I parted ways, though I had a feeling our paths would cross again.

I was truly inspired by Mike Love, Donovan, and of course, the Beatles, but now I had even more questions: What is this fourth level of consciousness? How is everything different? Can we really find peace by expanding our minds?

THE BRAIN AND TRANSCENDENTAL MEDITATION

Consciousness is life. If you don't have it, you're not alive.

—DAVID LYNCH

It was a lovely day in New York City. Spring was here and the cherry blossoms were coming into bloom. My friend Kurt Johnson, who's been in the spiritual movement for the past three decades, reached out and invited me to attend morning mass on the Upper West Side on September 11, 2001. This was the beginning of a ten-day event leading up to the Peace Day on September 21. He mentioned his friend Matthew Fox would be giving the keynote address and speaking on his latest book *The*

Hidden Spirituality of Men: Ten Metaphors to Awaken the Sacred Masculine. He thought it would be good for me to reconnect with him. When I arrived at the church that beautiful morning, I was surprised that the church was packed with people. Clearly, people were in tune with Matthew's wisdom teachings.

Listening to Matthew, I began to understand why our lives are so violent. "We have a distorted definition of what masculinity is," he told us. "It appeals to the reptilian brain, and we have to move beyond that to our mammal brains which are brains of compassion and kinship, family and bonding." Reptilian brain? What's that? "Part of our brains are ancient," he tells the crowd. "420 million years old to be exact. That's our reptilian brain. And reptiles make war. It's win/lose with the crocodile." Apparently, the journey to peace means we must calm the reptile within our collective genetic psyche. I'd heard him talk about the reptilian brain before, but I hadn't really understood. "We've got to mollify the reptile in us so that the mammal part of our brain—which is half as old, 210 million years old—can emerge. It's the mammal brain that is about compassion, family, kinship, and getting along," explained Fox.

I don't think Fox's message is about men coming into their femininity, so much as men detoxing their masculinity. For centuries, we have been fed toxic versions of masculinity telling us a real man needs to build an empire, whether that empire be a military empire, an economic empire, those great pyramids, or anything—as long as it is big. For centuries we've been told that's what you have to do to prove you're a man. What we need are other metaphors for masculinity, such as *the green man* for example—now there is an incredible archetype.

As Matthew explains, "The green man is about a relationship to the rest of nature. Men growing their beards and their hair are just a metaphor for the bows and the twigs and the plants of earth, and specifically growing from our mouth, as that is where the rest of creation starts to grow. You see, it's about our kinship with nature and other animals. That's what it means to be a man today. What are we contributing as men to the beheading of the earth and, therefore, to our children and their children whom we claim to love? We don't love them if we're not passing on a healthy and beautiful earth."

I could sense, listening to him, watching the crowd, in his being, a deep conviction and clarity for this truth to come forward. He continued, "We as reptiles love solitude; a snake, a crocodile, they love to lie alone in the sun. They do not bond but sit happily in solitude. So that's what meditation is; it puts us into solitude. It's how we befriend our crocodile nature. You befriend your reptilian brain so that the mammal brain can finally emerge. Every spiritual teacher that the world has produced, Buddha, Jesus, Isaiah, Muhammad, Lao-Tzu, Black Elk, all of them are calling us to our compassionate self, to recognize our capacity for compassion. Obviously, our species has fallen behind. We keep reverting to the reptilian brain, and when you also emphasize with men that the way they tend to prove their identity, their masculinity, is to win over someone else, to be number one through the act of conquering, to make war, be number one, eat your enemy— which is literally what a lot of our ancestors did in cannibal times and hunter-gatherer times—well, that energy is obviously war energy," explained Fox.

As the service concluded, Kurt grabbed me by the arm and said that Matthew Fox wanted to meet with us. Apparently, the topic of our documentary, *Rooted in Peace*, had garnered his attention and he wanted to catch up with my travels. I had so many questions. The three of us walked into Central Park and sat on a wooden bench as Matthew Fox began, "Compassion is a response to our being interconnected. To be rooted in peace, is to be rooted in the creative process of the universe itself." At that moment, I couldn't help but feel like I was in a movie scene from *The Hobbit*, and I was conversing with the great wizard Gandalf.

He continued, "Black Elk says that the real peace, the first peace from which all other peace derives, is about the human person being connected to the universe. When the psyche is connected to the cosmos, there is peace, because you know you're a part of a bigger drama and a bigger meaning than just our getting our toes stepped on or our egos wounded. There is a great peace that comes when you can breathe in the breath of the universe which is the sky—literally; the sky is what we're all breathing, and when you find your place in the universe, out of that peace comes the other expressions of nonviolence, of community building, of love, of healing that, of course, is so necessary for peace to return. It's like the Buddhists say: 'We're born in original peace and we come into the world yearning for this connection.' It's intrinsic to all of us, but it is a process."

As I listened, I began to realize consciousness is about waking up. It's about being aware of how vast our souls are, how vast our place in the world is, how beautiful it is to be here, and how brief a time we are here. As we walked out of Central Park together, Fox's comments led me to think about the Maharishi's fourth level of consciousness and how that meshed with this idea of quieting our reptile brains. As we walked out of the park, I said goodbye to both Kurt and Matthew and headed over to the newsstand. My eyes were drawn in as I noticed a man holding a brain. I picked up the magazine to see it was Dr. Dan Siegel, founder of the Mindsight Institute. The universe has an interesting way of communicating with you when you listen, so I took it upon myself to be in the conscious moment and see if he would meet with me.

As life would have it, it took about four days from the time I heard Dan Siegel speak at the Dalai Lama Summit for me to sit down with him in person. As I walked into his office to greet him, I observed from the corner of my eye his photos and credentials. Dr. Dan Siegel is both a family man, a well-respected doctor in his field, and an author. He'd published roughly thirty-some books, received his MD from Harvard University, and completed his psychiatry training at UCLA. Besides all the accolades, he also had a photo of himself and the Dalai Lama. I was curious why a leading author and psychologist would have a photo with the Dalai Lama.

I began the conversation by asking him about the roots of his Mindsight Institute. He smiled and began, "Mindsight is the term that refers to the ability of the human being to see the inner workings of their own minds or the minds of other people. It's a word that I made up at medical school. The Mindsight Institute studies how the mammalian brain (the prefrontal cortex), right behind the forehead, is the area we use to reflect on our inner lives." Dr. Siegel believes that's where the roots of change can be found.

Understanding some of what we do know about the brain can really be helpful. It should be done with the realization that at the same time we don't know that much about the brain, and we certainly don't know how the neuronal firing happens in this organ. Our brains are made up of a hundred billion neurons and their supportive cells, and each single neuron has an average of about ten thousand connections to other neurons, so it's a very complex organ with trillions of connections. Dr. Siegel explained, "I work in a field that combines neuroscience with a dozen different other sciences, and I work in a research center at UCLA where we deeply look at cultural evolution and how patterns of communication shape the synaptic connections in the brain.

"The simplest way to think about the mind is how some neuropsychiatrists have thought about it. They say the activity of the brain is the *mind*, a pretty common statement from a card-carrying neuropsychiatrist. Unlike the brain, a product of evolution, the mind is shaped by societal practices over generations. At the Center for Culture, Brain, and Development, we look at interpersonal neurobiology—or the way that human beings have embedded patterns of communication—which we call *relationships*. After all, a relationship is a way we share energy and information flow. This network, our social networks, include nodes, of course, the individual human being units, like families, larger units, like schools or communities, and it's all interconnected by the passage of energy and information flow.

"The thing we need to understand is that in the last three or four hundred years, one of the most important aspects of understanding our brain biology is that this brain continues to change throughout our lifespan. We used to believe when you're done with adolescence, your brain is done growing. We now know that that is absolutely not true. This brain is constantly redesigning itself. It's constantly responding to input that changes its synaptic structure. Once you realize this brain is incredibly social, and you realize it changes and responds to experience, and the experience we're talking about is actually how you focus your mind, then you realize there is incredible hope to make this a different planet. We have uniquely, in the human species, this part of the frontal area of the brain that is called the prefrontal cortex which is capable of using focus of attention to actually change its own circuitry. So, this is where consciousness permits choice, and change, and it's why we don't have to be on automatic pilot. You know, it's a natural thing from our evolution to just think 'I want to just take care of my little cave.' It's also a natural outcome of evolution that with awareness, we can actually change the pathway of our society."

He continued, "If you want to speak about the neural circuitry of love, one thing we need to realize is that a state of love is very much related to the circuitries that allow us to feel safe. In other words, if we feel attacked by someone, it's hard—because of the way we're wired—to feel love toward that person. If we shut down in fear, it's hard to feel love. If we're getting ready to fight, it's hard to feel love. And for a lot of people, when they feel helpless, they actually just shut down. And so instead of crying, they feel empty. Instead of feeling compassion, they just feel intellectual. In all these ways, whether you're freezing or frozen, in just helplessness, or whether you're feeling so frightened you want to run so you just turn away—that's the flight response—or you get so activated you want to fight, your instincts are dampening your potential.

"These circuits come from a much deeper part of the brain. These circuits come from the brainstem which activates a fight-flight-freeze response, and—depending on our individual history—we can either shut down and not feel anything, go numb, or we can get fearful and run, or we can get angry and start to fight back. And when you look deeply at how these brainstem areas interact with what are called the limbic areas—the emotional centers—you see emotion actually happens everywhere, and can work to drive our behavior in certain ways.

"These interactions are all below the cortex, where we believe thinking happens and awareness occurs, so we call them subcortical. The body feeds up to the brainstem, the brainstem then interacts with the limbic areas, and these subcortical regions push forward to make us think certain things. These basic chemical interactions give us the conviction that those people should be killed. We have conviction these things are really, really, really crucial, and that there's no other way to think."

He continued, "Reflective practices like mindfulness meditation or other mindfulness practices involve the higher areas of the brain and how they communicate directly with these lower areas. So rather than just being flooded by fight-flight-freeze, you shift your state into a more receptive state rather than reactive state, and that's the beginning of the neural process of love. You come to a situation with curiosity, openness, and acceptance, and that creates the foundation for love and that spells the word C-O-A-L. COAL: Curiosity, Openness, Acceptance, and Love is really the circuitry state of this network that allows you to thrive. If you think about how a chunk of coal is the origin of a diamond, it allows you to bring that diamond in the rough into a paradigm of changing our world. That's what mindfulness offers. That's what it means to see the mind as separate from the circuitry of the brain, and this mindsight approach gives us the ability to actually self-determine our fate.

"When you do meditative practices, like mindfulness meditation, you stimulate the activities of these areas, and they begin to grow," he told me. Grow? Yes. Grow. I used to believe that the brain stopped developing at adolescence, but today scientists have proven that it is elastic and is constantly changing in response to new input. As Dr. Siegel explained, by driving energy and information through the cortex, with controlled attention inherent in meditation, those areas of the brain actually get thicker and stronger—like a muscle.

"One of the implications of our research is that you are allowed to manipulate with your own intention, whether you live on automatic or you awaken your mind. You shift your state to a more receptive one rather than a reactive one. That neural process is the beginning of love, being in a state of love, and that state can change the world as we know it."

It was here, for the first time, I could see a pathway to peace. If there is indeed a peaceful part to our brains, and we could exercise it, like a muscle, we could accomplish anything.

He continued, "This idea of human heart consciousness can be understood in a deep way when you understand the nervous system. We have a part of our brain—the left side of the brain—that's extremely intellectual. It thinks in logical terms. It uses language and what are called digital representations. In contrast, the right side of the brain is much more closely connected to the body, and in particular, the viscera, the hollow organs of the body that have networks of neurons around them in spider web-like configurations around the heart and intestines.

"The viscera send up their signals through a layer of the spinal cord called the lamina one, or the marginal nucleus of the spine, which distributes data up through the spinal cord and actually brings these signals forward into the interior of the brain, not on our left side, but rather on our right side of the brain." At that moment, Dr. Dan Siegel was inspired and grabbed a mockup brain to show me. He explained, "In this right side of the brain, you have the frontal most area of the brain. It's this area that actually brings in the data from the heart and the intestines, called the insula, which makes maps of the heart. You can see from activation that the right insula is involved in empathy, as well as self-awareness. The key thing about heart wisdom is that it's not logical. It's not rational. It's not using language. It's literally a sensory experience of the body. This is where the wisdom of the body can change everything, because it's these right-sided bodily-based sensory experiences that allow us to feel for another person."

FEELING FOR ANOTHER PERSON

At that moment, with Dr. Siegel holding up a brain to explain the complexities of thought, I had a feeling inside me I couldn't explain. Dan was throwing a lot of information at me, and it was hitting its target. I started to look inside, and examine my reactive side and how I interact with others, especially my girlfriend, Britta. We moved in together about a month or so back, and lately she'd noticed that I'd become erratic and hard to communicate with. She described me as a "ticking time bomb waiting to go off." She could sense I was over my ears trying to finish this film, and was troubled by my finances. I was super stressed out. Here I was trying to find the answers to the world's problems, and now I was told that I'm supposed to focus on myself? I'd never seen myself as an angry person, or arrogant person, but I guess I was. I didn't want to acknowledge it, and I didn't want to change. But as Dr. Siegel spoke, I began to think about the last couple of months.

One afternoon when Britta had come home early, she could sense I wasn't having a good day. She was sweet, always smiling, and yet there was a point at which I just lost it. I was filled with rage. Why was I so angry? She looked at me and said, "I don't know what's going on and why you're driving me away, but I love you, and I want to help." I don't think Britta or myself knew what was going to cure my anger, or my constant upsets, but something needed to change—especially if I wanted to be with her.

I had read in a psychology journal in the waiting room of my doctor's office about PTSD and its effects. It sounded a lot like what I was going through. After doing some more research, I sought out Dr. Judy Kuriansky, who I discovered was a trauma expert, clinical psychologist, and representative at the United Nations.

When I met up with Dr. Judy Kuriansky, she told me, "Trauma is the result of people having been through some kind of experience that impacts them emotionally, and as a result they have a lot of feelings about that particular experience. Sometimes they keep it in, and sometimes they let it out, but it's an experience that can last for a very long time and that has an impact not only at the moment, and in their personal experience, but can spill over into every aspect of their life. To add to the complexity of trauma," she added, "there are three different levels of trauma. Generally, when people experience a trauma, it's because there's been some insult or some loss or perceived loss to the integrity of their being, or to losing a real person, or something that has happened to themselves. A personal trauma can come from a simple experience, like losing a cell phone, that someone else might say, 'Oh that's meaningless,' but to the person who lost the phone it could be extremely upsetting and disturb their world, so to speak.

"The crisis of trauma," she continued, "can happen on three levels: on the physical level, which manifests in real, physical symptoms that the person does feel, like aches all over the body, perhaps the person doesn't want to eat, has problems sleeping, has specific physical complaints like usually stomachaches and headaches; or trauma can manifest emotionally, where you just cry all the time, or you withdraw and feel that you're isolated and timid all of a sudden, or where you can be angry. The emotions can be all over the place. The third level is one of a spiritual crisis, where you wonder if in fact there is a purpose to life, or if in fact there is a God."

She was describing my life. We talked about how trauma affects our youth, especially in war zone areas, how children at different ages cope with living in warzones, and how they adjust with different kinds of mechanisms. You might have a five-year-old child who has to wear a gas mask who thinks, "Oh, this is fun! This is just like in the movies!" That's their way of coping given their level of cognition and their true psychological developmental stage. There are coping mechanisms, or defense mechanisms, that people manifest at different times, and a five-year-old child may cope with the kind of trauma of a gas mask or seeing dead bodies by thinking this is just what I've read in books or watched on TV and that might make the experience not as distressing for them. As a child matures, usually at about eight, children develop a kind of cognition as part of their normal developmental stage where they do know the difference between fantasy and reality, and so wearing gas masks, or seeing people who have no arms, or even getting an injury themselves, becomes potentially more damaging, the event more traumatic, because they do know;

'Oh my goodness, this is real. This isn't just something I read in a book.'"

As she was describing this moment, I started to cringe as it was reminding me of my time in Israel working on the Kibbutz and wearing my gas mask during the First Gulf War. Just talking about it triggered physical sensations, a rush of fear, a flush of anguish.

She continued, "Many adults living in a war-torn situation where there is tremendous carnage and horror that is happening, they disassociate, and they're not in the experience. It becomes like a fantasy, just as if a child is reading a story with images from a storybook. That's a way that the emotions cope with it. This is not really happening, it's not real, and the mind goes even somewhere up in the stratosphere, on the ceiling if there is one or up in the air, and kind of looks down on what's happening as if it is not happening to the person.

"That's called depersonalization or dissociation, a shock that happens so that you feel like this can't really be happening, because at one stage their mind chose to really cut off their emotions. It's called 'war shock.' Defense systems shut down, but eventually build up a lot of emotion, which often leads to an emotional outburst after the stage of shock has subsided. You get angry. Tremendous anger; anger at oneself, anger at the perpetrators, anger at God, anger at anybody. The flipside of war shock is that it may lead to depression or even becoming suicidal. Those two stages, depression and anger, flip-flop and last for a longer period of time. You get angry and then you get sad, and it can really change a great deal depending on the indi-

vidual. And then, over time, the final stages have to do with resolution. That is where most people come to say, 'Okay this happened, how am I going to accept it? How am I going to move
on? How am I going to live with it? How do I make sense of it
in my mind? How do I reconnect with myself, my feelings, and
with the people around me and even with my spiritual sense of
the meaning of life?'"

As she continued talking with me, she could sense I was
not comfortable with this conversation. At one point while we
were talking she looked at me and said, "Do you want me to
respond to your personal situation? I mean, this story is about
you. Right?" I didn't know how to respond to Judy at that moment. I was paralyzed, still frozen in the emotional state I had
stayed in for so long, but the one thing I realized was that I
wasn't alone. I was happy to know there is a logical progres-
sion, and that there are solutions.

She continued talking about post-war shock treatment and
how you approach people who have been through a trauma related to war. She said, "It's very individualistic. You need to be
very sensitive to the person's needs and their experiences. There's
no one-stop shopping out there about how to handle people in
war shock. The most important approach is to help the person
to feel safe again and show them that they are not alone." As we
concluded, Judy gave me a big hug. She sensed she had touched a
sensitive spot with me. Her last words were "good luck."

For me, that was the turning point. I realized I had anger
issues and, more importantly, my anger wasn't helping me. It
wasn't nurturing my development as a peaceful self, to connect

to others, to be an authentic person who can express oneself in a genuine unconditional way, with no attachments, no judgments. It was standing in my way of becoming a better human.

I decided to return back to Maharishi University, to attend the David Lynch weekend. I was super curious about this concept of Transcendental Meditation (TM), of redirecting the subconscious actions of my mind. My guide, and new friend, Ken Chawkin greeted me as I arrived and took me on a personal tour of the Maharishi campus. He seemed happy with me returning and for my new state of awakening to learn more about TM.

Maharishi campus was a world upon itself. The Vedic architecture found throughout the 40-mile compound were superlative. When building they considered the slope and shape of each area, how exposure to the rising sun would affect morning meditation, and built with green materials. There was some literature on campus that caught my eye talking about the Warrior Wellness program, and how Transcendental Meditation can heal PTSD, and I squirreled it away to read later. As we walked, he explained, that it was Maharishi's intent to have this institution designed based on the learning of consciousness. All the magnificent buildings I was admiring were built based on Vedic formulas, calendar readings, and astronomical settings. I was told that Donovan had asked for David Lynch to meet me privately later for an exclusive interview.

Our first stop was at the Center for Brain, Consciousness, and Cognition to meet Dr. Fred Travis. Sitting on a chair with a computer monitor in front of her was his daughter wearing a red electro-cap. It's basically a bathing cap stretched over her head with sensors to record brainwaves.

Travis explained, "What we're looking at here is the electrical activity of the brain. It's called an EEG, an electroencephalogram, and it's just the sum of all the electrical signals going on in the brain. What we're measuring is how the brain communicates. We think we communicate with words, but our brain cells actually communicate with electrical impulses. Depending on what you're doing, the brain frequencies will be different. What happens with the EE—as we can't go deep into the brain and touch the brain area like the amygdala which has been associated with fear or the whole brainstem reward circuit—but what you see is the overall functioning of the brain. What you find when someone is actually happy, you find the left front side of the brain is more active, because this is the part of the brain that sets up and organizes everything else. People who are depressed, what's happening is the limbic system comes up, completely grips the brain, completely grips their psychology, and their understanding of every interaction. It colors all existence. By looking at the total function of the brain, you can get insights into what the brain is doing, or rather how it is perceiving what you're doing.

"With inner wakefulness during Transcendental Meditation, we see frequency, high alpha waves. During Transcendental Meditation practice, the changes we can measure are primarily in the front of the brain. The front of the brain, it's the boss of the brain. It's that part of the brain which sets everything else up. The front of the brain has to do with decision making, judgment, sense of self, how to have more reasoning. It's really the higher cognitive centers of the brain. And what we see during TM practice is that in the front part of the brain, first, we see this appearance of an alpha frequency, so that means that part of the brain is not actively processing but it's still awake and alert. The reptilian brain is lulled to sleep and instead we see the connections between the left and right side of the brain are now more together, more coherent."

As Dr. Fred Travis kept explaining the intricacies of the brain and the impact of Transcendental Meditation, the one thing I observed was this deep sense of joy and happiness as part of his being. He was just so happy. I was full of questions. What was the mantra that could place you into a state of TM? How does it work? Can it really change one's moods and feelings? He answered, "Experience changes the brain, allows it to evolve, and so every time you go to that TM state of functioning of the brain, the brain begins to integrate it a little bit more. How long it lasts into your more active parts of the day depends on about how long you've been practicing TM. The longer you've been meditating, the longer the lasting effects of the activity, so there comes a point where you'll never lose the effect of this ground state of the mind, this restfulness, the alertness is there throughout the day, throughout the night.

"It's more than happiness," he explains. "We're living our life from a whole different space, and that is the ground of all experiences, this inner sense of fullness, of fulfillment, of unboundedness, of completeness, and this is how we process everything in activity. It's also how we appreciate sleeping, dreaming—and this is peace, this is real peace. Often, we think of peace as just the absence of conflict, but it's not. Real peace is based on inner fulfillment, inner fullness, where all of your actions are not a result of perceived deficiency, but are motivated by growth, a state where you want to help people around you. And this is what happens when you can bring the brain, and the consciousness, to that ground state where the mind is just full and awake and then we have a new basis for living life.

"Once we come to our full potential," Travis explained, "we'd become connected with our environment. In fact, we'll feel that we are that lively intelligence which is streaming through the environment all around us. We really see that the environment and us are no different. All is connected. Obviously we're different on the sensory level. I am here, you're there. But in a very fundamental way, we're completely united. That quality of wakefulness, of consciousness, and that desire to help the world is the same in all of us and both of us are just coming up in different ways, me as a scientist and you as a filmmaker."

"So, you're saying, if I'm understanding you, Dr. Travis," I asked, "that we're going to have compassion for birds and elephants as if we're all part of this great unified world?" Dr. Travis replied, "And compassions for ants and mosquitoes and everything, because everything has its place and so we appreciate the role each part plays relative to the whole. And again, it's not a cognitive act; it's on the level of direct experience."

After the interview, Ken and I went to the Maharishi University of Management cafeteria for lunch. Ken asked if I was aware of the unified field, and if any of this Transcendental Meditation stuff was making sense to me? I was open to learn and explore about Vedic wisdom. It seemed at first mysterious. Everything based on formulas, codes, mantras, energy. Their convictions were so solid. I mean, they even built an entire university on Maharishi's principles. As lunch concluded, we headed over to the Raj building where I met with Dr. John Hagelin, President of the Maharishi University of Management. As I was about to find out, Dr. Hagelin is a renowned quantum physicist and public policy expert, as well as an educator and a leading proponent of peace. He'd conducted pioneering research at CERN (the European Center for Nuclear Research) and is well known for his lectures on superstring unified field theory at Stanford's Linear Accelerator Center. I thought what better way to begin the conversation than by me asking him about this unified field. He was happy to fill in the blanks.

"The unified field is the unified source of the diversified universe," he began. "At the surface of life, we'll see incredible diversity, complexity. The deeper you go in your examination of the universe, the simpler nature becomes. There's the infinite diversity on the surface. There are tens of thousands of molecules. There are about a hundred types of atoms, and fewer and fewer elementary particles. The deeper you go at the more fundamental time and distance scale, when you look at the origin of the universe, at the most fundamental distance scale (the Planck scale) all the forces of the particles become one. This is the fulfillment of Einstein's dream to discover the unified source of the diversified universe. Today, that unified field theory is called Super String Theory, or M Theory, and it really reveals the scientific truth of the unity of life, which has been the essence of perhaps all philosophical traditions of the world.

"We are talking about a universal unified field of intelligence," he explained. "From this universal field come the particles, the forces, the whole universe unfolds. Now all the religions of the world, spiritual traditions of the world, talk about that fundamental unity of life. But today, modern science can confirm that, yes, at our core, you and I are one.

"Everything and everyone in the universe are united at their source," Dr. Hagelin continued, "and it's the ignorance of that, I think, that separates people. It is arguably the cause of tremendous problems, sufferings, and violence in the world."

Transcendental Meditation is the most ancient form of meditation in the world and the most profound. According to modern scientific research, it is also the most powerful.

"Very simply stated," Dr. Hagelin explains, "TM is a technique to turn the attention within. The normally outwardly directed attention actually starts to turn within to experience inner levels of far quieter, more abstract levels of thinking, and that inward flow of awareness quickly culminates in the experience of absolute silence, absolute unity, the direct subjective experience of the unified field, the direct experience of the unity of life. And that experience develops the brain more and more towards higher states of consciousness in which this truth of unity becomes a living reality in life.

"In the past," continued Dr. Hagelin, "scientific knowledge was not particularly profound. All the knowledge of the parts of our world were of their differences, of the uniqueness of the particles. Science today, however, is maturing to become more about the science of unity, the unified field at the basis of the diversity of our universe. Now that modern sciences uncovered the unified field in the context of Super String Theory and M Theory, we suddenly have a basis for discussion. A dialogue can open between the spiritually-minded and religious leaders of the world; because throughout recorded time, they've been talking about the reality of unity, the experience of unity, and until recently science has said, what's that? But now, with the discovery of unity as a building block of all of humanity, we really have a common ground for science and spirit to unite and come up with the real science of consciousness. I believe that science of consciousness, science of creative intelligence—that's here today."

Dr. Hagelin continued, "Maharishi Mahesh Yogi, foremost Vedic scholar of the world, has revived the whole Vedic science of consciousness. He brought Transcendental Meditation to the world from the East to the West, and revived it in India as well. Now, with modern scientists' working on a unified theory, we begin to fill that need for a complete science of consciousness, and this scientific study of higher states of consciousness has really come at the right time as modern science and ancient science shake hands in the unity of knowledge."

As Dr. Hagelin completed this last sentence, again there was another smile. Why was everyone so happy? Our conversation was interrupted as Ken peeked his head into the room informing me that David Lynch had arrived. It was time for me to meet the famous director. I thanked Dr. Hagelin, as he told me to call him John, and apologized for the short interview. He just smiled and nodded politely. Ken escorted me to the other room, where David had his hand out to greet me. There was an instant sense of calm surrounding his words as he began our conversation.

"It's the most profound blessing," David said, adding, "You know I've learned from Maharishi what comes from meditation, *Maharishi* meaning 'great teacher.' Rishi is a teacher, knower, or seer, and bringer of what you call total knowledge. Vedic knowledge is total knowledge. It's a technique that opens the door. The mantra you're taught and how to use it, the mantra turns that awareness within. You have to dive within, go to the ocean which is unbounded with totality, happiness, intelligence, creativity, energy, love, all there within every human being. But how do you get there?

"Maharishi's technique of Transcendental Meditation," Lynch continued, "opens the door easily, effortlessly to that. This is the profound. When you experience the transcendent, you infuse some of it every time you experience it, and so you are literally expanding your consciousness. That ball of consciousness is growing bigger and bigger, automatically. When you expand that ball of consciousness, and all those positive qualities, the side effect is that negativity starts to lift away from the human being. So stress lifts. Depression, sorrow, anxieties, worries, fatigue, hate, anger, fear start to dissolve and lift away. This is freedom.

"For me, the search began because I wanted to find that inner happiness," Lynch explained. "The thing that drove me was

I felt I had a reason to be happy on the surface. I had a reason to be happy, but when I looked at myself, looked inside, it was only a surface happiness. Then I heard this word 'enlightenment,' and I wondered if it is possible. Does a human being have this potential? It's a question. I just pondered this thing. It seemed like, maybe in the East they thought this crazy thing, but I never heard of it in the West. I truly believe that a human being has a huge potential, for enlightenment, fulfillment, liberation. I had these anxieties and worries and doubts. I had a lot of anger. Then two weeks after I started meditating, my first wife comes to me and says, 'What is going on?' And I said, 'What are you talking about?' She says, 'This anger, where did it go?'

"Maharishi says anger is a sign of weakness. It's a weak thing. An angry person is a weak person. They can't handle something, so they get angry. It poisons the person, and it poisons the environment. Given this technique, you can dive within, and unfold that. Happiness comes, sadness goes away. Depression lifts; hate, anger... all this negativity restricts. Consciousness is life, if you don't have it, you're not alive." David paused to see if I was following him.

"There is a thing. This ocean within has many qualities, even though it is oneness, it has various qualities. One of those qualities is love, and there is an infinite amount there within every human being—infinite love. You start experiencing that, and living that, infusing that, and bliss is love, love is bliss. Everybody has this experience of this falling in love and having it reciprocated. She loves me, and I love her, and isn't it the most beautiful world? But love doesn't require another.

"The world is as you are," Lynch continued. "And that love and that happiness and that energy and that intelligence—that is also called 'dynamic peace.' The unified field is ten million times ten more powerful than the atomic level of creation. It is a huge infinite power, and when you enliven it, it moves isotropically at the speed of the light. It sees no barriers, like a bright light of peace radiating, lifting negativity away. It affects all avenues of life. Unified field is bliss consciousness."

As we concluded our meeting, David asked how my meditation was going. I was a bit embarrassed as I had not yet received my mantra. It also took David by surprise, but he smiled and said he would take care of it for me. After the interview, Donovan met up with me and a bunch of Maharishi students to plant a tree. Now this was right up my wheelhouse, and we both thought it would be symbolic of my new peace journey to be putting a new sapling into the ground. We would grow together.

All I can tell you is that within two weeks of beginning my new TM practices, everything started to change. It became completely apparent that TM could help me alleviate my anger, fears, and anxieties. It was an inspirational weekend for me. I received my mantra and learned how to meditate, which began a whole new way of life for me. My inner self was shifting. The fog had lifted, and my relationship with Britta had begun to heal.

A VISIT TO HEARTMATH

As many poets have said for eons, the heart appears to be the main access point to the wisdom of a higher self, to what we call heart intuition.

—DR. ROLLIN MCCRATY

As I began my Transcendental Meditation practice, my life slowly started to shift. I was becoming less erratic and more stable. I had a much deeper sense of awareness around me, personally, socially, and professionally. For one thing, I had a deep sense of an awakening, a feeling of my inner self expanding. I was also clearly falling in love with my girlfriend, Britta. I had just returned from a retreat up in Mayacamas Ranch with one hundred spiritual like-minded leaders. At the conference, I met up with social entrepreneur Terry Mollner, who coincidentally also lived in Amherst. He was smiling as I began explaining my inner journey and this new sense of being that I found through my newly found Transcendental Meditation practice. At that moment, I was like a kid in a candy store learning about the various forms of meditation, mantras, and techniques that exist in the world—Hindi, Indian, Jewish, Arabic, Native Indian traditions. He was keenly aware of Maharishi Mahesh Yogi and mentioned that he had heard him speak for the first time when he visited Amherst College in 1973. Maharishi talked then about this expansion of the mind during mediation, and this new sense of awe, a new sense of being.

As we walked out on the patio, looking over the horizon in the Mayacamas Mountain Valley, he asked if I was familiar with an organization called HeartMath. He thought they would be helpful in my expansion of learning about different forms of meditation, one of them being the heart. He mentioned that the *Scientific Journal* recently published a new article about the HeartMath Institute, stating, "The heart may be more powerful than the brain." He thought it would be inspirational and life changing for me to meet two of the founders of the organization, Dr. Rollin McCraty and Dr. Deborah Rozman, up at the Institute in the Santa Cruz mountains. There has always been something soothing about the Santa Cruz landscape, and the suggestion seemed fortuitous, so I took him up on the offer.

It felt like just another road trip. I woke to the beautiful blue ocean in Marina del Rey. My relationship with Britta was beginning to bloom, and she was also curious about this HeartMath Institute, encouraging me to head up north to Santa Cruz to visit. Along the way up the Big Sur coastline, I looked over the most breathtaking views of the Pacific Ocean. My heart was pounding. I was in love. It took about an hour to finally get up the mountain and arrive at the HeartMath Institute. Rollin was a happy older gentlemen, who looked to me like the movie star Will Ferrell, though a bit nerdier. We walked into the lab together, where I observed a wire contraption with computer monitors stationed throughout. It felt like we were entering a deep space nine probe. As we went farther into his lab, he sat me at a station, placed some wires on my head, and said, "Breathe. Focus on your breath moving through your heart. Control your feelings."

Dr. McCraty emphasized that the heart is much more than just a pump. "As many poets have said for eons, the heart appears to be the main access point to wisdom, to the higher self, to what we call heart intuition. We've always believed that the brain controls the heart, but that's a myth. The heart sends much more information to the brain, telling it what to do, than vice versa. With every beat, the heart emits an electromagnetic field five thousand times stronger than the brain's. The heart and brain are designed to be complementary. The idea is to get them to work together."

I agreed to have my heart rate variability (HRV) tested in the lab. As I was being hooked up, McCraty explained, "HRV is the beat-to-beat change in our heart rate. This is very different than heart rate. Heart rate is just how many times does the heart beat in a minute. But in a healthy individual, somebody who's healthy and resilient, our heart rate changes with every single heartbeat and what's really interesting is the time between these beats—if you look at it over time—the heart's beating out a message, literally a signal that we can detect. What we found in our research is that the pattern, or the message that the heart rhythms beat out, is very much related to our emotions and how we're feeling."

Once I was wired up, Dr. McCraty explained, "We measure the time interval between each heartbeat to show one's HRV. Negative emotions—frustration, anger, and anxiety—create incoherent, jagged rhythm patterns. But, when we're enjoying heartfelt qualities of genuine kindness and love, the heart's rhythm becomes smooth and orderly—and becomes a sine wave which is called a coherent pattern. This state maximizes our mental functions."

As Dr. McCraty continued talking, Dr. Deborah Rozman entered the room and began to chime in. "Well, the same thing is true of our body. When signals in our nervous system are out of sync, we're burning a lot of extra energy. We're draining our resilience and our vitality unnecessarily. On the other hand, when we're feeling sincere, heartfelt, positive feelings, we're really caring for someone, or we're having that true compassion about a situation in the world with someone, whether it's appreciation or forgiveness—with these types of genuine heartfelt feelings, the heart beats out a very different message and it creates what we call a coherent pattern. And as it turns out, this coherent heart rhythm is the key to the physiology of optimal function."

To begin, they engaged me in heart-focused breathing, putting my attention to the center of my chest, and breathing from there. Next, I consciously activated the feeling of love I shared for Britta. Immediately, my HRV shifted. Literally, the machine lit up. The variability had moved from low coherence to medium coherence. And, when I said out loud, "Britta, I love you," it moved into high coherence. Amazing!

Dr. McCraty explained, "Being angry, even for a few minutes, sets in motion 1,400 biochemical changes. Some of our stress hormones have a half-life of twelve hours, so a single upset can have long-lasting effects. Most of us have gotten to the place where incoherence is the familiar so it takes some time to rewire the neural circuits. But it can happen … with some practice.

"HeartMath is basically a system of tools, techniques, and technologies that allow a person to better self-regulate themselves in a more intelligent inner-reference place," continued Dr. McCraty. "We're able to make better decisions in life, to handle stress, and increase our resiliency when we come from a centered base. Our minds are as different as are our cultural beliefs, up-bringing, and intellectual capabilities, but we all feel, and we all have the same desire for love, care, and kindness. These qualities of the heart make us all the same—part of the same tree."

Dr. McCraty and I continued with my heart-based breathing for a few more minutes, while Dr. Rozman expanded on the definition, "HeartMath is kind of like an oxymoron. Most people go, 'Heart and math?! How do you put those two together?' But really, HeartMath is about the 'unfoldment'—a step-by-step process that has been scientifically validated of opening and connecting with your heart. It is about learning how the heart and brain communicate with each other, and that there are pathways of heart, brain, and nervous system communication to be explored that are based on science, physics, and neuropsychology."

Dr. Rozman was quite persistent in this area and very well-versed. Furthering my education, she continued, "A lot of people think of the heart as Valentine's Day or those kinds of more metaphorical type things of the heart. Doc Childre, Jr. coined the term 'HeartMath' and we mean it quite literally when we say the heart has intelligence. It's intelligence we can draw on and access, so that's where the math comes in. Through psychological equations, we learned very specific techniques and steps to access what we call 'heart intelligence.' You really can access, or draw on, our higher capacities in ways that increase our performance in many areas of life, including our health.

"Doc Childre, Jr., the founder of the HeartMath Institute, wanted to take the idea of our 'heart' out of just the metaphorical or poetic or spiritual connotation and give it some anchoring and grounding. He felt that those expressions *play with your heart, live from your heart*, and *follow your heart* were not just sweet things to do but a guide to better living, and one that could be quantified and roadmapped. Learning about that model is really an important aspect of our unfoldment as human beings, one that has physiology and psychology and mathematical elements of science, so to speak, behind it," she concluded.

She was teaching me to think of my heart like a radio-receiving transmitting station. She emphasized that as a psychologist her viewpoint was much different than that of a scientist. She explained, "The psychological aspects of things, and what we have seen in the research, is that as we are feeling/emoting, whatever we are experiencing is actually like a radio transmission that affects our perception of reality. It is what we put out in that electromagnetic field that shapes our world. The heart's electronic field can actually be measured if you record the electronic feed coming from the body with traditional scientific instruments, whereas the brain's field can only be measured maybe an inch away from the physical brain itself. It is our understanding that these two centers of electronic charges, these two organs, are actually designed to do different things in a complementary fashion simultaneously.

"The breakthrough research at HeartMath," continued Dr. Rozman, "came when we discovered the critical link between emotions, emotional state, and the heart's rhythmic beating pattern, and the fact that you could look at the heart rate variability, the rhythm of the heart, and see different emotions in it—frustration, anger, or anxiety, each had a different pattern. In physiological terms, what we call negative emotions—stress emotions—these states of being really angry create incoherent, jagged heart rhythm patterns. When we are feeling heart-felt qualities of a genuine kindness, love, care, compassion, or appreciation, the heart's rhythmic pattern becomes smooth and ordered and more like a sine wave … which is why we call it a coherent pattern."

I was in awe of what Dr. Rozman was telling me. Clearly she was a master in her field of psychology, but this point of view, talking about emotions in terms of mathematic equations, was fascinating. "Now what the research showed is that the heart's desire is actually settled in the brain," she explained. "It tells the brain how the body is feeling with that emotional pattern and the brain responds to the heart's input. Our paradigm for thousands of years is that the brain controls the heart, but what we are finding out is that is not true. In fact, the heart sends more information telling the brain what to do than the brain tells the heart—this two-way communication process goes on enabling us to connect with the core values of our heart, like deeper respect for each other, love, kindness, all the heart-based qualities that make us connect with each other."

"So, does that make us human?" I asked.

She replied, "Human, yes, but it also informs the brain and can actually open up higher cortical functions in the brain."

Dr. Rozman continued, "It is what we call heart intelligence. When the heart and brain are in sync, and we can see it visually in an actual line, that is what happens when you get into this deep heart coherent state. In that state, even what you are saying is more aware, more conscious, more connected, more intelligent and we call it heart intelligence because the heart is really driving the process. It is that intuitive discerning heart we seek to make friends with, to become our standard state of being."

I guess one can say the heart is the ultimate power station, not just physically as an organ beating all the time, but emotionally. It is a place where we can start to really learn self-regulation. We can take charge of ourselves and learn from the heart how to tune in to its guidance. That's the key piece. Dr. Rozman asserted, "How to tune in to that intuitive discernment, that comes when the heart and mind are in that alignment that's the key. Our goal is to become clear as to how our higher self, or larger self, or connection with our source, whatever you want to call it, can be accessed more as we dig deeper into the understanding of that part of our being."

"So, the heart is like a portal to higher consciousness, to bringing together all our centers and systems in alignment, right?" I asked, adding more to myself than to her, "We really can become more of who we really are, more of our authentic self." Knowing this, I realized I had a lot to learn about referencing my heart, reflecting on times when I get upset or stressed, and, when that happens, connecting back to that heart center.

Dr. Rozman smiled, "You can make heart-based living part of your life and you will see that your world comes more into alignment, that you feel like you are going with the flow, life will seem more convenient, you'll experience more creativity, more fulfillment, and here and there is an opportunity for us to empower ourselves … for your true self to unfold."

I began to sit more comfortably in my chair as Dr. Rozman was guiding me through her cognitive process and some emotional exercises. "Well, the key thing here is the individual. There are a lot of different reasons why we handle stress differently. There are genetics, there is diet, there is exercise, there is attitude, and there is a lot of data showing that stress (both emotional and anxiety-based stress) have a big strain on the heart. Our focus at HeartMath has been to look at the pathways of communication between the heart, the brain, and the nervous system and how emotional stress or emotional peace affect the heart physically, but also affect our perceptions in how the heart and brain work together.

"My experience, when people connect more with opening their hearts, with the love in their hearts, and allow forgiveness to take hold, is that the heart heals and the stress symptoms dissipate, while at the same time we see an individual's health drastically improve. Participants are also motivated in the alignment to do what they need to do to improve their behavior, to make necessary changes needed to experience a better life. For example, we have a program called 'Stopping Emotional Eating' in HeartMath. We look at stress eating or emotional eating as a missing x-factor in why a lot of people go yo-yo dieting, lose some, gain some or can't keep weight off or can't stick to a diet. The emotional component is often not addressed. Weight is related to food, it is related to exercise, but we often don't address the motivations that keep you eating, or in some cases eating unhealthy food. It's even deeper in some cases; it stems from self-worth issues, or emotional attitudes or what's mentally behind it. Some people need to get to the root of these issues before they can break that dieting cycle."

My heart was controlling my weight? This was interesting. "In our six-week program," she continued, "what we found in the beta test is that after a couple of weeks of doing this, people naturally have the feeling of wanting to eat differently, wanting to go to the gym. They are coming in sync within themselves and they are motivated to make other behavior changes that their own heart was guiding them to, but they hadn't been listening; hence they transition from emotional eating to more intuitive eating or heart-directed eating. In simple terms, the heart is providing a new landscape of learning in any aspect of life, relationships, food, education, learning, career path choices, and general fulfillment. Our hearts are there to remind us of our authentic self. So, the terms 'follow your heart' and 'listen to your heart' are right on. If you go deep into your heart for the answer, all issues in life have physiological underpinnings enabling us to connect more with our real potential self."

What Dr. Rozman told me is that they have found, at Heart-Math, that the best time to use these tools is in the morning before you start your day. Specifically, they recommend "heart locking" before you go out into the world, which is a type of heart meditation where you get into a state of heart coherence, you focus on radiating love, or appreciation, through the electromagnetic field of your heart and projecting it out to our planet. "You want to get to a place where you are emanating and expanding your conscious sense of care and love and expanding that to a much wider expansive field with your intention focused on staying connected to your heart. Unlike some traditional meditation methods, you should not get off too much into visualization, or stay too much in your mind, but rather keep that heart coherence steady within your system."

Seeing the wave monitor in action as I guided my thoughts from one loving memory to another, I could see the affect intentional emotional thinking had on my well-being in a quantitative way, perhaps for the very first time. As we were finishing up, Dr. Rozman handed me a box with an emWave monitor inside it. "It's for you. A gift for making the drive up to the Santa Cruz mountains." I was humbled by Deborah's gift. I could feel in her heart a deep compassion for me and my heart's journey to find inner peace.

"EmWave technology keeps us honest," she warned me. "Through this simple hand-held device, you'll be able to measure your emWaves whenever you want, as it allows you to measure your own heart rhythms. You'll be able to monitor yourself and tell how coherent you are. It gives you an objective way of visualizing and seeing when you practice some of the HeartMath self-regulation techniques. Instead of asking, 'did I make that shift into the coherent state or into that optimal state?' you'll know for sure, by reading the coherence of your rhythms. They'll never lie."

What I've learned is that beginner meditators find it hard to still their minds. They may spend half their meditation time wondering around trying to get still. EmWaves show you when your heart arrives in that special coherent place with either sound feedback or light feedback. It allows you to start expanding your real heart intention deeper and deeper within your meditation. It trains you to get there faster.

Dr. Rozman, Deborah, was vibrating with happiness throughout our visit. There was so much to share. She taught me that the heart is the central intelligence of our nervous system and our overall well-being. Instead of repressing or attempting to deflect emotions, it was important to embrace the energetic levels because you can feel the negativity or the other stress on the other end, but it is how you perceive what is coming into you that affects your overall well-being. We are constantly under attack by stimuli. It's how we perceive that stimuli that determines the underlying effects all of that has on our psychophysiological being. Being in tune with our thoughts and emotions and how they interact with human physiology is imperative to our unfolding. Again, stress—a lot of people don't understand what stress really is—it's always an emotion, an emotional response. It's the anger, frustration, irritation that we experience. When left unguided, it depletes our inner energy resources.

On my ride back, I listened to the recordings of our interview and was able to process even more. "Our real empowerment," said Dr. Rozman, "is whether we are able to respond to our everyday stimulus in a way that is productive, healthy, creative, and aligned, or whether we are instinctively reacting to them, and, by doing so, triggering the fight/flight downward spiral of judgment, resentment, and blame, which keeps looping around on itself. These simple tools and techniques allow individuals to better self-regulate our energy expenditures which in turn allows us to maintain our resiliency. But it's important to also understand that this coherent state that I'm describing maximizes our mental functions as well. By just shifting from a normal state into a coherent state, that alone increases our reaction times on average about thirty-seven milliseconds. That's a huge deal when you're talking about neural processing speeds," she continued, pulling out statistical data to support her claims. "For example, let's say you're a baseball player. You're up to bat and the pitcher throws the ball at 90 mph. If you can shift into a coherent state, you perceive it as slow as 80 mph—it's that big of a difference—so that's a pretty big factor. The tools and techniques we're teaching help build and sustain resilience to increase our ability to stay in charge of ourselves; to manage our anger, our frustrations, which can be very influential when these types of emotions exist in very challenging contexts and situations.

"And you talk about rooted in peace," she continued, "I mean, the things in my world, where we learn to change your heart rhythm pattern and how we study how the heart and brain perceive reality and talk to each other, those are your roots. The profound changes we see when we switch to non-judgmental thoughts, switch to forgiveness, switch to care, genuine care, and kindness, those are the qualities that root me in peace, that enable me when I don't feel peaceful to find that peace. It comes from my own interalignment, comes from my own heart. Our scientific studies show that peace comes not from what happens outside of me, but literally from our own hearts.

"My heart becomes like my compass or GPS guiding me in the direction I want to go," Deborah tells me, on a personal note. "By practicing these mindful techniques, and testing them out over time, practical intuition has become more and more ingrained in me. It becomes clearer. I call it heart guidance. You now have more energy to do what is fulfilling. You seek to expand your awareness and be more creative. These heart-based techniques take a conflict and resolve it on another level of resolution. We grow through conflict, and learning how to take conflict as an opportunity for growth requires that heart connection; because really, what are you in conflict about? Is it perceptions, beliefs, what are you conflicting, what are we in a disagreement about? Our identities, our beliefs, our desires? Really we all just want to feel that we are actually the same. When we don't see that we are already the same, that's where conflict comes. We both want to have opportunity to grow and learn and love and connect, so really, we are already alike."

"These needs and feelings expand beyond our inner selves," interjected Dr. McCraty. "Our energy fields are interconnected with global energy fields and for the first time we are studying the relationship between the two. To that end, there's the GCI. The Global Coherence Initiative, which is a science-based project, has set out to really measure and understand how the earth's energetic systems interact with human emotion and consciousness to help offset the planetary stress wave. We're installing a global network of earth monitoring stations that are specifically designed to measure what I call the energetic fields of the earth—the geomagnetic field. That's the field our compasses tune into.

"If you think of the earth here," Dr. McCraty says, miming a globe, "and it's got the magnetic north and south poles, those magnetic field lines don't just circle the earth, they go out many, many thousands of miles into space around the planet. It's a stationary field like you have around a bar magnet—the field's always there. The magnetic field of the earth is actually critical for life on earth. It's our main shield from what's called the solar wind. The solar wind is made up of the particles blowing out of the sun travelling through space at about a million miles per hour. The force of the solar wind is enough that it literally pushes the earth's magnetic field in on one side and pulls it way out on the other side. Without that shield, there would be no life on earth."

Dr. McCraty continued, "If you think of these magnetic field lines as guitar strings, they're very much like that, even though it's considered a static field or a stationary field. The field lines get plucked as they interact with the solar wind and vibrate and have resonant modes just like a guitar string does. As it turns out, those vibratory modes, vibrating magnetic fields, overlap the human heart, the frequencies that the human heart operates on. In fact, one of the primary frequencies of the earth is the same exact frequency as the coherent heart rhythm, that optimal state for human performance. There are actually a number of frequencies in this range, frequencies the earth manifests, that overlap the cardiovascular system."

So this measurable coherent heart rhythm, the one associated with times a subject thinks of unity, peace, acceptance, and forgiveness, is the same as the frequency that earth's magnetic fields vibrate on? Illuminating.

As I drove through the countryside, listening to the session I had just experienced, I wondered if I could actually feel that field around the earth. I imagined I was a station receiving the signals of the universe. Could one hear the planet's guitar strings being plucked by the solar wind, if you really listened?

Rollin interrupted my thoughts. "Now the other energetic system that our sensors are designed to measure also exists around the earth, and it is another shield, also a mystery of life on earth. It's called the ionosphere. It starts about fifty miles up from the surface of the earth and goes out to about two hundred miles. This is a dense layer, a highly charged dense layer, basically made up of ions, referred to as a plasma. There are very strong current flows travelling around the ionosphere. They're very complex patterns, a big figure-eight spanning globally across the planet—around the earth and so on. And whenever you have a flow of current, a flow of energy, you create magnetic fields—that's a whole other source of magnetic fields that are being generated on a planetary scale by the planet itself.

"There's a cavity between the surface of the earth and the bottom of the ionosphere and the ozone layer that creates a resonate chamber. A lot of people know the stories about amateur radio operators—often called ham operators—who talk to somebody on the other side of the planet with their equipment. What they are doing is bouncing their radio wave off the ionosphere. So it goes off, and bounces off the ionosphere, and goes around the planet so it has that resonant chamber. There's a whole other set of rhythms that are globally propagating waves that are with us 24/7 that are in this resonant chamber, and they overlap exactly to the patterns of human brain waves. That is to say, we have planetary magnetic fields vibrating 24/7 that operate in the same regions or realms as the human heart and another set that are almost exactly overlapping patterns put out by the human brain."

This scientific discovery is illuminating. We, us, globally, vibrate at the same frequency as our planet. First of all, it is a quantifiable way of understanding that we are fundamentally interconnected with each other and the planetary system itself.

Most importantly, they claimed changes and disruptions in the earth's energetic systems regularly affect us in a mass way that correlates with our human emotions.

Rollin explained, "When the planetary fields are incoherent and disturbed, our tendency as humans, globally, is we trigger easier, we're prone to getting more upset and quicker. The biggest part of our human physiology takes the brunt of our emotions. We get mentally confused, fatigued, more anxious, and quicker to anger, frustrate, and become irritated easily. It plays out in real-life scenarios in increased traffic accidents, more criminal activity, more hospital admissions—more war! It's like in theater when there is increased drama, except on a planetary scale.

"There's a graph," Rollin explains, "that was published by a very famous researcher who was the first to observe these correlations. It was first published in 1926. And if you saw the graph, your mouth would drop open. It looks at the number of major human events back to 1749, and overlaps the solar cycle, looking at the planetary geomagnetic influences on human behavior. They're exact overlays. The results are undeniable. We are profoundly influenced by the magnetic environment we live within. Now, what we're also suggesting through the Global Coherence Initiative is that it is a two-way street. Not only are human emotions in physiology affected by the planetary energetic systems but we affect it as well. Our human capacity, human feelings, can be measured and reflected in the planetary energetic systems. It's really a bi-directional or two-way street."

Here I had been trying to figure out how to plant the seeds of peace, so that a fundamental message of freedom and light could grow and spread all over the earth, and it turns out my heart was a megaphone the whole time. Could this really be true?

"Tracking this data," said Rollin, "helps us understand how a relatively small number of people coming together—who have really practiced being more coherent—can help stabilize the planetary fields; facilitating the awareness and the consciousness of all living systems within the larger planetary fields."

At this point, my curiosity was piqued. I wondered if days humans collectively celebrate, like national holidays, show up on the graphs. I heard myself asking, "Do you measure national holidays like Father's Day or Mother's Day, or international holidays like Christmas?"

"No," he explained, "but we do measure occurrences like earthquakes that are triggered by a large scale of emotions being triggered at the same time."

"How about the tsunami in Japan? What did you see from that?" I asked. Rollin took a deep breath and continued "Let me say it this way: some of the strongest data showing that humans have an impact on planetary magnetic fields actually occurred during the terrorist attacks of 9/11. There's a very sharp, stark shift in the planetary fields, and then you see total incoherence in the fields for the three or four days afterwards. These are planetary skill fields I'm talking about. I mean, there was a lot of fear and anger all in a collective or mass kind of consciousness, that was strong enough to show this influence. And measurable! What we're actually measuring is the earth's geomagnetic fields and these ionospheric fields. And mass pain and terror measurably seem to affect those fields."

"It's energy? Can we tap this energy?" I interjected.

"Well," Rollin chimed in, "magnetic fields are magnetic fields. I don't know how else to answer that. What we're really looking at is showing the interconnectedness between human consciousness and human emotions and earth-level, earth-scale fields; in other words, we're wired together. And this is really important, because it means that every individual counts."

This was so profound and so directly related to my search for peace, my concern that I was just one person. What could I possibly as one person do to make a difference on a global scale? Here was a scientist telling me the data says I do count. That my very thoughts and attitudes of the world around me can affect change. My mind was blown. A lot of times people will tend to think "I'm just one person," but, in reality, every human on the planet has the same capacity—we all affect the field. It doesn't matter how rich or poor you are, or anything like that; we all affect the field equally.

After this moving discovery, I began a practice of taking stock of each of my personal reflections on a twenty-four-hour cycle. I like to ask myself at the end of the day questions like, "How much of the time today did I spend being frustrated or angry or wrapped up in my to-do list versus really being more caring and compassionate, really appreciating my day?" I try to look back at each week at the end of the week and review where I chose to put my focus. Was it on me, perceiving blocks and obstacles, or was it on others, and how I could be of service, make a difference, bring a smile. Because we're putting out those energies, those fields, and it's the total of all humanity that creates the planetary consciousness and now, for the first time, I am completely aware that I am a part of that total.

That's what Global Consciousness Initiative is really all about, just helping educate people that our thoughts not only matter but that we actually have a choice. We don't have to be influenced and tossed around, so to speak, when the planetary fields are upset. We can learn to self-regulate ourselves and put out a more coherent field especially during those times. I became aware that doing so helps others find their balance, their composure through those more challenging times. When I center myself, when I unfold, when I use HeartMath to balance the electromagnetic waves I project, those waves bounce off the ionosphere, reverberate globally, and the result is a better world.

Before I left the institute, we all walked out on the balcony to experience the sun setting. I was happy, feeling powerful, smiling, filled with joy. My heart was beating, but in a new profound way. I was part of the universe. My heartbeat was part of humanity's collective heartbeat. And more to the point, I felt deeply connected to the wonderful being that was sharing my journey with me, Britta. I gave both Rollin and Deborah hugs and headed into my car.

Driving south down the 101, I remembered that Mike Love had given me a special present that he asked me to listen to. After listening to the insight I had gathered from Rollin and Deborah, I placed Mike's CD into my car stereo player. I remember he had mentioned that the song he was giving me had sat in his archives for the past fifty years, that it was written during the time he met George Harrison, and that it had been written for George. It was called "Pisces Brothers." The lyrics and sound pierced my soul.

Chills ran through my spine as I listened to the music. My heart was pounding for Britta. My brain started asking questions like, "Why now? Why me?" I swept those thoughts away, incorporated my mantra, and focused on the love I felt for this amazing woman in my life.

SEEKING HEALTH
IN A TOXIC WORLD

We face a global emergency. A deepening climate crisis
that requires us to act.

—AL GORE

My mind was awakened, and my heart fully embraced my relationship with Britta, but unfortunately my body wasn't operating on the same mode. I was beaming out love and light to the
universe, but I was also sick. It began with a throat infection
that just wouldn't clear up. After calling and seeing the doctor
three times, and him prescribing the same prescriptive medica-
tion, Britta and I started to get nervous. Conventional medicine
wasn't working, and I needed to find a remedy—quickly.

Browsing the internet, I discovered Dr. Mark Hyman and his TED Talk on functional medicine. I was unhappy to learn how I had been misled about antibiotics. In fact, Dr. Hyman said they are the single biggest false turn in medicine. "It gave us the impression that we could treat all diseases," he explained through the light on my computer screen, "feeding us the idea that we could simply kill this offending agent with a single drug—the magic bullet theory."

Unfortunately, when you're sick, a complex system is thrown out of balance. As Hyman explains, "Physiology and biology are connected, not only to what's going on inside you, but also outside you. Functional medicine, on the other hand, connects the dots between our biology and our environment. We need to figure out our biological terrain, not just the bug. We need to look at the body in the context of our unhealthy planet."

I decided to make an appointment and visit Dr. Mark Hyman out in the Berkshires of Lenox, MA. Prior to my visit, his assistant, Anne, informed me that I needed to visit a blood clinic and give some blood and stool samples. I got a bit nervous at the clinic after the fourteenth vial was filled. It seemed like a lot of blood just to understand the complexity of the body and my imbalances. I wondered how much I had left. Plus, I was told the bloodwork would not be covered by my insurance. Yikes. I thought that was a bit peculiar as this was a "general health and well-being analysis." Apparently, our insurance systems are set up to treat the symptoms but not look at the cause.

Meeting Dr. Mark Hyman at his office in the Berkshires seemed like any normal doctor's visit. He had numerous diplomas on the wall, including his college degree from Cornell University, medical degree from the University of Omaha, and master certificate from the Institute for Functional Medicine. He was quite tall, friendly, and asked me to forgive him ahead of time as he had many complex patients that day, which made him late. I was grateful he had made time to meet with me. This infection had gone on for too long and was affecting my ability to be productive.

"The body is an ecosystem," he began, "and when it's out of balance, disease occurs, symptoms occur. When you create health in that ecosystem, disease goes away as a side effect. You don't have to actually treat the disease by itself to achieve balance; you can treat the body as a whole and achieve the same desired effect. At a certain point, one must ask what are the things that actually drive imbalances in your body and what are the things that create balance. It's a short list. There are very few things that create imbalances: It's diet, it's stress of all kinds—physical and psychological stressors, it's allergens, it's toxins, and lastly it's microbes that affect your biology."

He continued, "I started treating diseases as I was trained to do so in medical school with medications and I realized, in many cases, that people weren't getting better. I thought perhaps there was another way to think about medicine—looking at the underlying cause of disease and how it affects our biological systems. As we're looking at healthcare and how it relates to medicine, the thing that's emerging in the sciences is a very simple idea: that our body is a complex ecosystem, and we have to understand how it works, what disturbs it, and what creates health. It's something we never learn in medical school. Diseases become irrelevant as we understand the underlying causes. We understand how to get rid of those causes and support the health of the body by enhancing its function with basic raw materials required for health. It's quite simple actually: Take away the bad stuff and put in the good stuff, and the body knows what to do."

I was curious what had led Dr. Hyman down this path to search for other causes to disease and what triggered his journey. For one thing, he looked extremely healthy. In fact, he explained, "I had always been rather healthy, but when I lived in Beijing, I got sick, often. It turns out I was reacting to the enormous amounts of mercury in the air, the coal burning, and I eventually used an air filter to help with the problem. I'd clean the filter every day, but while outside I was still breathing in the coal-soaked dirt and dust the inhabitants of Beijing are all too familiar with, and that had huge amounts of mercury in it. After a while, my system couldn't handle that, and I broke down. And dealing with that, attempting to find solutions to my illnesses, really helped me understand the connection between the environment and our health and how truly linked they are."

Dr. Hyman continued, "We don't understand that just since the turn of the last century, we've had eighty thousand chemicals introduced into our environment, most of which have never been tested on human beings. Eighty thousand. We don't realize that typically there's 287 known neurotoxic chemicals being found in the umbilical cord blood of the average newborn. That means the baby, before it's even taken its first breath, has flame retardants, pesticides, phthalates, bisphenol-A, mercury, lead, and arsenic, all in its blood. How does that impact our children?"

Wow. Here I was, concerned with my own health. Now I'm concerned with the health of future generations. If Britta and I have children, what toxins are we subjecting our children to? And their children?

"It's our diet, our standard American diet, what we call our SAD diet—just processed, low fiber, high sugar, low vitamin and high glycemic food, which we've found drives all the pathways of disease," says Dr. Mark Hyman. "It's stress, which includes psychological stress and media stress and toxic stress—there's all sorts of stress—which drives imbalance. And there are environmental toxins, things that we are exposed to every day. It's our makeup, our skin care products, our sun blocks, our household cleaners, our food, fish which contains mercury, arsenic in our water—these are all real toxins that are affecting us every single day, and they impact our health. Allergens, which are common, and things that are even more common like slow-grade food sensitivities, which drive inflammation in the body—unrecognized for the most part; things like gluten, which affects almost twenty million Americans, but it's mostly undiagnosed. It can drive tremendous inflammation."

For the first time, I was beginning to really think about that old axiom "garbage in, garbage out" and how I might have been poisoning my own system by simply not paying attention. "Your fork," Hyman continued, "is therefore the most powerful tool you have to change your health. You vote three times a day with your fork. You vote not just for your health, but you vote for the environment when you choose the sourcing of your meals. When you eat, you're also voting for what's happening globally in our world. The choices each of us make every day, three times a day, are the single most important choices we make every day about things that are going to impact our health and the planet every single minute. What most people don't get is that sustainability of their health is connected to the sustainability of the planet. You damage your health, you're damaging the planet. You damage the planet, and you're damaging your health.

"Remember," he continued, "you are made up of microbes of all sorts. Some of the biggest and most important microbes are not the ones that cause infection you and I know of; but they're the microbes in your gut. That microbiome, which makes up one hundred times more DNA living inside you than of your own body's DNA—there's ten times as many bacterial cells in your body as there are your own cells. Plus, the drugs we use create more than side effects, they spawn bad bugs, drugs like antibiotics, acid blockers, steroids, and hormones of different sorts. What we'll be doing together is looking at the totality of the input you place in and on your body. And then of course, there's genetics, which play a role, but it's a very small role. All of those insults affect our body. They influence our gene function and create imbalances—imbalances that invite disease."

At this point I was starting to get nervous. Dr. Hyman took the tests and placed them on the table. "In your blood tests, you have a blood sugar level that starts out pretty normal at 96, although that's not really normal. An optimal blood sugar is approximately 70–80. If we did your waist-to-hip ratio, we are going to find that your waist is bigger than your hips, and you have belly fat," concluded Hyman.

He was right. I was obese. I had too much belly fat—the kind that sends hormones and inflammatory molecules into the bloodstream, creating a cascade that leads to premature aging and death.

"When I look at belly fat," Hyman explained, "what I think of is a stressed-out person. Belly fat accumulates under the influence of cortisol—a stress." He also told me I have high cholesterol and I was pre-diabetic.

And he wasn't done, adding, "You also have a few other problems." At this particular juncture, I asked him to change his vocabulary from "problems" to "symptoms." It sounded better and felt like something I could tackle, rather than just live with. "Well, you have imbalances that need to be fixed," came his answer. "Whatever you're eating is reacting with your immune system because your gut is not healthy. 60 percent of your immune system is in your gut to help fight against foreign invaders. In there's bacteria, food, proteins—all a cell away from each other—being dealt with by your immune system. Toxins in our environment, coupled with lifestyle choices, can weaken your body's immune system and can trigger disorder.

"This professor at Harvard MIT," Dr. Hyman shared, "was a bioengineer and told me about a study where they analyzed the teeth with mercury fillings in them. They found out that mercury goes down through the dental tubules into the bloodstream, as well as vaporizing off the top of the tooth over time."

Not only was my gut unhealthy, but I started to think about all the ways my lifestyle choices could have caused this irritation. I started to think about my dental fillings. Were they made of mercury? Did that "solution" in my mouth leech to the linings of my gut?

Dr. Hyman smiled at me, "Mercury is the most toxic non-radioactive substance known to man. When dentists remove it, it has to be disposed of as hazardous waste. How is it safe to have this in our mouth?"

Walking out of Dr. Hyman's office, I felt distressed, overwhelmed, and angry. Why hadn't my normal internist informed me of this analysis? Why was I spending three hundred and fifty dollars for a general check-up every year? What had they been checking? I'm a toxic mess. The whole medical system seemed upside down and disjointed.

After Dr. Mark Hyman's visit, I ventured down the road to visit my alma mater, the University of Massachusetts at Amherst, and meet up with my colleague and friend Chris Kilham, the author and educator known as a medicine hunter. He's conducted medicinal plant research in over forty-five countries. Perhaps he would have some insight into my never-ending throat infection.

"Plants are our true medicine," Chris tells me. "I would define true wellness as the complete integration of body, mind, and spirit with the past, present, and future. I don't think you can separate personal wellness from social wellness, and I don't think you can separate those from the quality of our environment. I think we're one unified planet where the path to actual wellness is broad, thorough, and completely integrated. I'm not really interested in symptomatic relief. I'm interested in people having happy, joyful, healthy, beautiful integrated lives. That's wellness.

"Toxins, by definition, challenge and operate counter to the natural expression of life," Kilham continued. "If you breathe toxic materials, that degrades your health. If you drink toxins in water, that deteriorates your health. If you have agricultural toxins in food, that harms your health. Toxins take away; they don't add to health and wellness. Oddly, most of what we consume, and the areas we live in, put us into contact with a wide array of pesticides. Pesticides, toxins that are used on food crops, are by definition intentionally poisons. They are designed to kill life. They're designed to kill insects. They're designed to kill worms. They're designed to kill beetles. But all of these creatures have living cells and reproductive systems, and we share the same make-up, the same biology, with all of these types of creatures. So, what's toxic to beetles and worms and insects is toxic to you and me. Pesticides, fungicides, and other agri-poisons that actually deteriorate our health can be found to increase rates of cancer and other very serious diseases.

"The answer can be found in history," Kilham continued. "Hippocrates said, 'Let your food be your medicine.' Of course, you have to have pure food for that to be possible. We know from repeated studies, including studies conducted by the national academy of sciences, that poisons intentionally applied to food crops are responsible for higher rates of cancer and cancer mortality. There is a direct link between what gets put on our food and whether we live or die. That's a real serious equation. That's not a frivolous thing. That's not a notion of the privileged. That's something that runs to the very core of our existence."

Kilham was in full soapbox form at this point, and I was happy to eat up the knowledge. Up until now, at mealtime I ate what I felt like eating. I grabbed, ordered, or shopped with very little thought as to the origin of my food or what pesticides might have been used or what the quality of the water was where my food was grown or had lived. But it turns out, quality of food matters. Anything we put into our bodies affects our biology.

He continued, "And don't be fooled by organic labeling. Certified organic foods are still going to have some environmental toxins in them because everything has environmental toxins, but at least they won't have poisons intentionally applied to them, and so in choosing organic food we reduce the risk of various degenerative diseases."

I'm realizing, as he's explaining this way of looking at food choices, that organic isn't just trendy, it's really important. It's even important to the long-term health of our soil. It turns out farmers who work with agricultural poisons have about seven times the rate of different types of cancers as the general population. That's unwarranted. Why should farmers be dying of cancer? They don't have to if they're cultivating crops organically. That simple change could reduce that risk for those working in our food growing industries. So organic isn't just a privilege we get to choose at the supermarket; it's the way food should be. So now, added to my list of things I need to do to save the world is to buy organic and encourage others to do so. It turns out it's a matter of life and death.

We talked for some time, Chris and I, about food sourcing, and the miles food travels before it gets to you, and all the issues involved in polluting as we tend to plant far away from where we live. Then he pivoted back to plants as medicines.

"A medicine is,in theory, something that helps to promote, restore, and maintain health and balance within us," he explained. "Plants are the largest category of medicine in use in the world. The plants call to us. I go into places like the Amazon or Siberia or the mountains of China, or the deserts in the Middle East, wherever, and work with people in those regions to understand their traditional plant remedies. High-value plants that stimulate healthy heart or brain function, or increase sexual drives. For example, the native people in the South Pacific have a special plant called kava. Kava has been extensively proven in human clinical studies to help relieve anxiety, and given that you have about nine million Americans on the anti-anxiety medications of the big pharmaceutical companies, using a plant alternative is not a bad idea.

"I've worked with *rhodiola rosea* from Siberia and Northern China," Chris continued. "Extensive clinical studies show that it's beneficial for the brain, for energy, endurance, and stamina. It's probably the single best antidepressant agent in any category in the world that will pick you up, establish better vitality and mental clarity, and make you feel good. But in this country, traditional medicine hasn't even heard of it.

"Cacao, as it turns out, is probably the ultimate superfood," explained Kilham. "The agents in cocoa, in cocoa beans, turn out to be profoundly beneficial for the heart, reducing the risk of heart attack and stroke and high blood pressure and hardening of the arteries. They're very beneficial to mind and mood. They enhance brain function. I think we're at the beginning of a kind of a cocoa revolution in which cocoa makes the transition from being a favorite candy, and a sweetened one—sort of a guilty pleasure—to a real lifesaving medicine." I was very happy to hear chocolate was still my friend.

"Açaí, another superfood, comes from the Brazilian Amazon," continued Kilham. "It's a palm fruit, it's purple, and it's used to make juices and smoothies and sorbets and all kinds of things. Those purple pigments are insanely beneficial to the immune system and also have anti-inflammatory properties. The antioxidant activity is very high so it protects us and keeps us healthier and youthful. That's an example of a real high-value fruit. There's a vast body of science on açaí. So, any time you're consuming açaí, you're going, 'Hey, great snack,' and your body's going, 'Wow, I'm getting this walloping load of concentrated, super healing nutrition with every bite.' It's a good equation."

After all this talk of beans and berries and chocolate, I was curious what a traditional breakfast looked like for Chris. "Okay," he says, "this morning my breakfast was a chopped apple, a sliced banana, a handful of cashews, a handful of almonds, two dates, and a couple pieces of whole grain toast. If you put clean, nutritious food into your body, then your cells and everything about your body gets to function and benefit. If you put in garbage food, if you put in high calorie food that doesn't have much nutrition, you don't satisfy the needs of your body and your health. You wind up fat, tired, depressed, things don't work right, your digestion is lousy. You go to real natural foods, preferably organic, unprocessed. I mean, great food. If I had you at home for dinner, you wouldn't say, 'Wow, this is weird food.' You'd say, 'What a great meal.'"

Chris talked about the large corporations who are raking in billions of dollars on products with ingredients like high fructose corn syrup, and cheap starches, and fatty meat—companies that are foisting genetically modified food products on the American public—and he was clear that these companies are reaping great economic rewards at the grave and horrible expense of the health of the American public. "Why do we consume 70 percent of the world's antidepressant drugs," he asks, "when we have less than 5 percent of the world's population? Why are we the fattest nation of people on earth? What the heck is going on here?

"You know," Kilham mused, "Buddha said that the cause of human suffering is ignorance. I think people are bullishly ignorant. Right now, environmentally, it's the norm to poison our environment. It's like we're sitting in our living rooms happily watching television while our bedrooms, bathrooms, kitchens, garages, and basements are completely on fire. We are bewilderingly oblivious of the obvious. We are destroying the natural environment, every parameter of it we're deteriorating, and we don't seem to realize that as the environment goes, we go too. I don't understand how people can fail to realize this in a concrete way that moves them to do something. But I think it is the norm that most people just feel separate from nature. It's completely delusional. That's the sad thing. It's so obvious that we're inextricably intertwined with all of nature. And so, to offend nature, to degrade nature, is to offend and degrade all of humanity as well."

Listening to Chris, I started to think about health and wellness in a whole new way. I really had spent most of my life oblivious to the obvious. Specifically, the chemicals and elements we extract from the environment and put into our bodies. The first step of my wellness program was to remove those silver dental fillings, partially made of mercury, out of my mouth. I sought out an alternative dental hygienist who uses a special dental procedure for extraction, ensuring none of the mercury would leak during removal.

I then linked up with a local nutritionist in Los Angeles to help me get my body back in balance. I started observing what I put in my mouth and reading labels at the grocery store. I know GMO is a super controversial subject, though I find it hard to believe that our government doesn't actively and more thoroughly mandate what corporations can put in and on our products. I decided to continue my education on this topic, and met up with Deborah Garcia, the wife of Jerry Garcia, and one of the founders of the organic food movement.

When I arrived, Deborah was cleaning off some fruits and veggies she had just gotten from a local farmer's market. They were bright and crispy, and as she spoke, she handed me healthy snacks, encouraging me to feel the freshness. "There's two competing food systems," she began. "There's agriculture and there's agribusiness. There's the corporate one that's completely anonymous, synthetic. Products can be on the shelf for years—that's basically fake food. When I started researching what was going on in agriculture, I soon learned about genetic engineering. Genetic engineering that is 'recombinant' uses DNA technology. It's where they break apart DNA, and then they recombine it with DNA that is from another species. They put bacteria in wheat, or human genes in fish, or they put genes from fluorescent jellyfish into rabbits. They recombine it, using a certain technology that uses viruses and bacteria as delivery systems—it is a cell invasion technology. With recombinant GMOs, we actually change the very nature of the cell. What they've learned since they started bringing out genetically engineered crops is one gene change does not create just the one desired trait—making a plant able to withstand drought, or making it grow taller—but it can create all kinds of additional traits depending on its environment, side effects if you will."

Deborah explained that the concern with genetic engineering is that what we are letting out into the world is mutating; pollen is taken in the wind, and then crossing with other species in the wild, and you often lose control of the original DNA.

"You really don't know what kind of toxins these things may be creating," she explained. "It's about integrity. A cell has its integrity, and a species has its integrity too. We have to honor that integrity, and if we come with our scientific techniques and say, 'Oh, you know this is supposed to be a pig, but actually we are going to put a whole bunch of rat genes in here, well, then you have really damaged the integrity of the gene. And at whose cost? We have no idea. It is not like—with genetic engineering—you can just pull it back. That's the root of the problem. There are all other sorts of issues around the science as well; who's patenting, and who controls the seed that we are now transforming? The whole process is based on true arrogance, and it is actually very, very dangerous.

"Our society is soil blind," continues Garcia. "We take the soil for granted. We think it is inert. You know, it is just this brown stuff down there called dirt, but that's not true at all. Soil is alive. Soil is a system. It is an ecosystem. There are billions of different kinds of organisms in it, and they all have relationships with each other. The plants have a relationship with the soil; the roots have a relationship with the fungi in the soil, and that in turn has a relationship with the rocks that bring the nutrients to the fungi that bring it to the plant.

"The biggest thing that nature is teaching us is that nature gives back. If you look at a forest, you know nature; the forest is a perfect ecosystem. You know the nutrients go up into the tree and into the leaves. The leaves fall off down to the ground, and then they are broken down by microorganisms, and they go back into the soil, and they feed the tree. Nature gives back. It is a system that has its integrity."

I was in awe of Deborah's commitment to the organic movement and her determination to bring the truth forward about soil integrity. I let out a heavy sigh. We both instantly smiled at each other and hugged, as if we had known each other from a past life. We were on the same mission. I knew I was with a truth seeker and the source of, or the mother of, the organic seed movement, and I was grateful.

I realized understanding food was an integral step toward me achieving health, wellness, and balance. In the weeks that followed, I removed GMO and industrialized foods from my diet and incorporated superfoods into my daily routine. Stress was a culprit too. I knew that. High cortisol levels, a result of stress on the system, can impede fat burning, metabolism, and hormone balance. So I got a trainer, Eric the Red. Besides my exercise routine to wake up my cells and support a healthier metabolism, I added some boxing techniques in the gym. I developed a habit of practicing a morning and evening Transcendental Meditation. I started taking a probiotic before bed to aid in my overall digestion, as well as adding some antioxidants that were beneficial to the immune system into my diet, enhancing anti-inflammatory properties, which also brightened my mood and heightened my brain function. It was all about making healthy decisions, changing my mindset, making better choices, and opening my heart. It was amazing to see my body, well-being, and relationship transform over time. I was beginning to feel new inside and out.

As I continued my health exploration, I realized I wasn't alone. Many young people throughout the United States, and the world, are sick. After Dr. Hyman's wake-up call, I met up with Dr. Alejandro Junger of the CLEAN program, who had had the same unhealthy experiences I had gone through, only here in my backyard of New York City.

"I started getting sick, I started having allergies, and I started having something called irritable bowel syndrome," started Dr. Junger as we sat down in his Topanga Canyon home office. "But it was only when I started waking up with this sense of impending doom, that later on was diagnosed as depression, that I consulted a psychiatrist, a gastroenterologist, and an allergist in search of the underlying cause. I was left with three diagnoses and seven—*seven*—prescription medications. It just didn't make sense. The inspiration behind CLEAN was my quest to look for a solution for my health issues that did not include *seven* prescription medications, *seven* chemicals in order to function every day. I took off to India to study Ayurvedic medicine and other forms of healing, began taking natural supplements, and started getting better. It wasn't until I discovered cleansing and detoxification, and I became aware of the pervasive attacks of toxic chemicals in modern life, that things began to change for me."

Dr. Junger explained, "We are organisms that were designed by nature, just like the rest of the animals in the world; and when animals live according to nature's design, they don't get sick. There are no monkeys in the wild with depression, or rhinos with irritable bowel syndrome. Animals in the wild live, eat, reproduce, and get killed by an accident or by another animal. They die of old age. It is when animals, like us, are extracted from their natural environment that we start getting sick. Modern life has taken out all the natural conditions from our life, and that's why our organisms are reacting and defending themselves against this barrage of chemicals that we daily consume in the name of modern life.

"Most of us are aware of global warming and the inconvenient truth that it represents," explained Dr. Junger. "But global warming, if you look at it from a doctor's point of view, is just a symptom; it's a fever. What is causing the fever I call another inconvenient truth, which is our global toxicity. This global toxicity is causing a fever. The earth is like an organism. The rivers are like its arteries, forests are like its lungs, the internet is like its nervous system. You and I are like two red blood cells in your body. We are a part of this organism, and we are sick.

"When you look at an organism that has cancer," Dr. Junger continued, "you study those cells, and you see they are killing each other and killing other cells. They are producing toxic chemicals that they're releasing into circulation that affects the whole organism. They also like to travel and conquer distant places—and this is exactly what human beings are doing right now. It may be that we are the cancer of this organism—the planet.

"Peace is an inner state, it's like software," Junger explained, "and for software to run properly, it needs the correct hardware. Our hardware, our organism, is in a state of defense. It's reacting against these chemicals; it's reacting against the conditions we live in, against our relationships. We are stressed; we are defensive; we are afraid. But these emotional states that we are experiencing translate also into a biochemical state of inflammation and irritation. And that is what our cells are doing constantly—they're defending themselves from this attack from our environment. An organism that's in full defense cannot, by definition, experience a full state of peace. At the most basic level, we are made of atoms and molecules that are re-acting and playing this game of physiology. These molecules, these atoms, they come from food; every single atom in your body came from food. We literally are what we eat.

"Now, if there are things, if there are molecules that your body needs that you are not eating," Junger continued, "then there's going to be things that are missing in order for your body to achieve its optimal function. Not only that, if some-thing is missing, the body will try to compensate in a different way—so it will spend energy and resources trying to adapt and compensate for whatever is missing."

Junger added, "The other aspect is that not only are things missing, but other things are coming in, which are not only not useful but toxic. For example, there are molecules that come in and bind to other molecules, and together they don't allow oth-er useful molecules to enter the game; therefore, it is as if those molecules were missing. They can't get absorbed. Now, either things are missing or things are being blocked by certain obsta-cles. When you remove the obstacles, and you add whatever is missing, everything corrects by itself as if by magic. The body's always constantly trying to do the right thing, and it knows how to do the right thing, but it needs certain things. It needs the obstacles to what it needs to be removed. Now, if there are things that are missing, the body cannot do certain things, so it will adapt and do other things in order to compensate—this is what's going on. We have so many toxins blocking the nor-mal physiology; and we have so many things missing because our soils are depleted, because we take the food before it's ripe so that we can transport it for thousands of miles in trucks to the supermarket where they're going to be sold before it spoils. In the process, we are missing things, and we are adding things that block our organism from working correctly.

"We have encyclopedias of medicine describing diseases," continued Dr. Junger. "There are symptoms listed, and grouped into syndromes, that are grouped into diseases that are coded and named and are given protocols in order to treat them. My idea is there are no diseases. The body is perfectly reacting to its environment; and what we call diseases today, it's just a survival mechanism that we are witnessing.

"For example," Junger explained, "I'm a cardiologist, and everybody knows that heart disease is what's killing 50 percent of Americans today; part of heart disease, or the biggest aspect of heart disease, is what doctors call 'coronary artery disease.' What is coronary artery disease? It is the deposit of plaque in the coronary arteries that feed the heart. Now, if you were able to make yourself little and go inside the artery, you would see that the artery gets irritated, it forms a crack as it were, and the body perfectly tries to survive this insult by patching it up with cholesterol. Now, in nature, insults come and go, storms come and go, earthquakes come and go. But in human modern life, insults persist—so the arteries crack, the body patches it up, the arteries crack again, the body patches it up again. If it were in nature, the insult would disappear, and the artery would reabsorb this plaque—this has been proven by Dr. Dean Ornish and many others—that arterial plaque is reversible. If the insult disappears, the cracks should disappear, and if the irritation disappears, the plaque itself would be reabsorbed. But in modern life, the insult persists—so more plaque is being deposited, more plaque is being deposited, and although the body's just doing its perfect work of survival, once the plaque gets thick, it prevents blood from flowing. We call that coronary artery disease. But that's not a disease. That is the perfect survival mechanism that our organism is born with. What the disease is, is our lifestyle. What the disease is, is the irritation that the artery is trying to survive—so we have it wrong, there are no diseases. Mostly, there are mechanisms of survival that, when they persist for too long, end up killing us.

"Now, the different foods that I propose that people eat more of are for different reasons," Junger explained as he drew up a plan for my CLEAN program. "Some of them, like garlic, are good because they are antibacterial, and they will eliminate the bad bacteria in your gut. Others, like olive oil, have anti-inflammatory properties, anti-inflammatory nutrients that will appease the barrage of inflammation, the upheaval of your immune system in trying to defend itself; because one of the things that is missing from our diet is all the anti-inflammatory nutrients—the most famous one of which is the omega-3 fatty acids or fish oils. Those are missing from our diet, and you'll find that when you reintroduce them to your diet, your immune system will calm down. This is the reason why many of these nutrients are allowed and are highly suggested you consume, while doing a cleansing and detoxification program, like the CLEAN program. This is the reason why we would prescribe them."

I asked Dr. Junger what his inspiration was in creating the CLEAN program. He shared, "I wanted to experience life normally. I wanted to be able to function. I wanted to be able to go throughout the day without sneezing and getting my eyes watery and infected. I wanted to not experience this bloating and gas condition that every food made me experience."

After our conversation, I went online and purchased his CLEAN program. It was a twenty-day intensive cleanse that Britta and I did together. We each lost about twenty-plus pounds. We noticed more color in our skin. Our resilience, health, well-being, and stamina were optimum. It was a complete reboot to the body. It was just the renewal I was looking for.

I was on a path to find personal health and optimum consciousness. Change, I learned, starts from within. I was beginning to realize how even our individual health related to global awareness, and the future health of our big blue planet. As I left Dr. Alejandro Junger's home, the last thing he said stuck with me, like a puzzle. He quoted Einstein, saying, "You can't solve the same problem using the same kind of thinking you used when you created them."

I wondered what he meant by that...

HEALING THE ENVIRONMENT

The atom bomb did not wake people up about warfare, famines haven't woken people up about poverty and food, epidemics haven't woken people up about disease, and now the devastation of the natural environment has not woken people up about environmentalism.

—CHRIS KILHAM

So change began from within, and I was making changes—lots of them—but how did my health relate to global awareness, peace, or the future of our planet? Perhaps Deepak Chopra put it best when he said, "We are one climate; we are one ecosystem;

we are one economy; and sooner or later we have to realize that we are one humanity."

But that realization can be slow in coming. As Chris Kilham said, "So many disasters, and still the people sleep." I'm actually not convinced that there is a wake-up call that'll suddenly make people go, "Oh my goodness, we have to change." And that apathy is a terrifying prospect!

When I was still at Amherst, Al Gore's book *Earth in the Balance* changed my life. It opened my eyes to the dangers ahead, and it activated my inner activist. And now that the earth gave me back my health, his message resonated even louder. I'd always been deeply concerned about the health of our living planet and the reality of the climate crisis, and I'd even had a chance to attend the inaugural Clinton Global Initiative, where I listened to former Vice President Al Gore speak to a packed audience. He was enflamed, filled with vigor and purpose. He stood at the podium and shared his findings with deep conviction. Gore's message was simple: "We face a global emergency, a deepening climate crisis that requires us to act." But that message went largely unheeded, resulting in his next documentary, *An Inconvenient Sequel,* which calls for the same awakening, rings the same bells, and sets off the same alarms. For instance, we lose 0.5 percent of forest yearly including 0.1 percent to deforestation. Kathy Abusow, CEO of the Sustainable Forestry Initative, says "Deforestation is a contributor to greenhouse gas emissions globally. Forests really do have a vital role in storing carbon."

I had a chance to sit down and meet environmentalist and world-renowned green architect William McDonough, who told me, "We don't have an energy problem in this planet right now. We have a material problem, which is carbon. Carbon gives us life. We are carbon ourselves. But what we have to realize is that we have carbon, a material, in the wrong place: the atmosphere. And because of that, 43 percent of the carbon produced by humans since 1850 is now in the oceans. We're now witnessing their pH levels drop to the point that we expect that we will lose the bottom of the food chain. By the end of the century, coral reefs will dissolve to the point where we will lose the bottom of the food cycle that feeds everything." What we've created is essentially carbonic acid.

Fabien Cousteau, grandson of famed Jacques Cousteau, tells us that the seas are the circulatory system of life. "Whatever happens to the oceans quite literally happens to us," said Fabien when we met up. "It doesn't matter whether you live near an ocean or whether you're thousands of miles away. Ocean acidification is one of those backlashes that is the result of the chemical change that happens when CO_2 is absorbed into the oceans.

"You know, being a Cousteau is not a gene. It is a philosophy," mused Fabien as we sat down during the Blue Mind Summit in San Francisco. "We all need to have a little bit of that philosophy, that Cousteau philosophy in us," continued Fabien, "because, at the end of the day, being an environmentalist is not about being green, or being an extremist. It is about a mantra—or an essence—of who we are, and what role we play on this planet. We need to see our environment as a natural bank account. We need to stop eating away the capital and start living off the interest.

"A healthy environment is a healthy economy," continued Cousteau. "Most importantly, I have great hope for human beings. If we were logical about our resources, we would not be doomed. The key question is, 'How can we protect something that has no borders?' We have to understand that this planet is a singular model. It's not land *or* sea. It's not two different planets here. This is one planet. It's one life support system. It's the circulatory system of life.

"We aren't surprised when an addict shoots up, their veins are full of poison and they get sick. It is the same thing with the circulatory system of life—our water planet—which is the water in our oceans, lakes, and streams. We dump things like coal ash, or nuclear waste, or DDTs and PCBs and flame retardants into our great expanses of water. Now it's a plastic soup out there. A floating reef of garbage. One spans from 150 miles off of California all the way to 100 miles off of Japan. Now that is the length of Canada, that is huge. We are talking about 1.5 million pounds of plastics that are dumped in our oceans every single hour of every single day. It is not just in the North Pacific. There's a garbage patch in every ocean. There's one in South Pacific, the Atlantic, the Caribbean, the Mediterranean, and it is only getting bigger by the day because we are not addressing the root problem, which is our use of the oceans as garbage dumps. Our oceans will continue to be sick as we continue to keep accumulating those plastics. We shouldn't be surprised that not only are the fish getting sick, and morphing, and having several eyes or genitals or what have you, but we shouldn't be surprised that human beings are now starting to exhibit those same issues; because at the end of the day we are dependent on that global food web for our very survival."

Listening to Fabien made me think. How could I approach the cleanup of our oceans in any sort of manageable, meaningful way? What could I as one person do? I was deeply concerned about the exploitation of carbon in the atmosphere, and how we as global citizens could ban together to resolve this escalating problem. It wasn't just a climate crisis, but a health crisis waiting to go off.

If you look at the symptoms of climate change, those we already see, it really brings the most devastating impact to the planet, the worst injuries. But hearing Fabien's belief in humanity, I was still hopeful. Perhaps together we could still right this ship, turn our focus, stop the madness.

There was one organization, founded by Richard Branson, whose approach was completely revolutionary in design. Branson's initial point of view was if we've got something so devastating immediately upon us, all you have to ask is, 'What would Winston Churchill do?' Well he would start a war room. His thinking is you bring in the smartest people you can find, and you actually have them input all of their information into a central place, and you make decisions together on how to prioritize efforts around tackling this big problem.

Jigar Shah was Branson's new CEO, leading up the Carbon War Room. He had just returned from the front lines of India before sitting down with me. He looked frazzled and war weary as he explained where they were in the process. "When you look at global climate change," Jigar began, "you start seeing climate refugees that are coming out from Bangladesh to places in India, to farmland that has increasing desertification. They arrive in a place, like in India, where 50 percent of the entire population, which is a big number, works in agriculture; at the same time at which you start seeing water shortages and desertification, and all of these other impacts, like the influx of refugees looking for resources. Then you start to see fear, you start to see unrest, you start to see some of these things that nobody really wants to have occur. And what's scary is people don't exactly know how to fix it. Climate change is really measured in terms of parts per million of CO_2, carbon dioxide in the atmosphere. For a long time, we were at 200 parts per million. We're now closer to 350 parts per million because of all the coal that we're burning, and some of the other things that we're doing. As a result, it seems unlikely that we can stay below 350 parts per million, which means that we're probably going to have temperature levels around the world go up by more than two degrees, which we know will continue to cause sea level rise. That, in turn, causes all sorts of dislocations of individuals, it causes a lot of hardships. More refugees. More stresses on existing systems. More fear."

"I think you need to make it real to people," says board member Jean Oelwang, CEO of Virgin Unite. "I think right now we almost got our knickers in a twist by using the word 'carbon,' and the words 'climate change,' when the real root cause is that we are depleting all of our natural resources at an incredibly swift pace."

After conversing with Jean Oelwang and Jigar Shah at the Climate Summit, I decided to make my way up to the capital building, in the heart of the city of Washington, DC, to meet up with world environmental thinker Lester Brown, founder and former president of the Earth Policy Institute and founder of the Worldwatch Institute. Brown is the author or co-author of over fifty books on global environmental issues, and his works have been translated into more than forty languages, his most recent, and hopeful, book being *The Great Transition: Shifting from Fossil Fuels to Solar and Wind Energy.* I had lots of questions, and it was clear this was a much bigger problem than most of us understood. As I put out my hand to shake Lester's, he was already engaged in the conversation. "Warmer today than the average. The temperature is rising, and that brings all sorts of changes. The higher the temperature, the more evaporation. Because of the more rapid evaporation, you get more moisture in the atmosphere. You get more rainfall. You get more destructive storms, hurricanes, and tornadoes; because you have more energy in the system. What's discerning is that we live in a technologically advanced, highly organized society; however, we somehow think we are independent from the economy's natural support systems.

"We are as dependent on forests and soils and aquifers and grasslands and fisheries as the Sumerians and Mayans," explained Brown. "If we continue destroying these natural resources as we are now doing, then eventually our economy will also decline and collapse. Take, for example, when you fuel up your car. Every gallon of gasoline you burn increases the amount of CO_2 in the atmosphere. This is what is driving global warming. And when we talk about the costs, we don't include things like treating respiratory illnesses resulting from poor breathing conditions, or that we're living in the polluted air as a result of burning gasoline. When you look at all these costs, when you really factor in the true cost, a gallon of gasoline cost not $3 a gallon, but $15 a gallon. Those are the real costs. Fossil fuel costs at the pump plus the cost of medical expenses to treat the results from burning those fuels. Someone is paying for those costs. We pay these costs in increased health care costs, or when we deal with the destructive weather consequences of climate change. Either way, we're paying a premium price.

"The whole system is changing, and one of our biggest problems is dealing with our agriculture issues and preventing a food crisis," warned Lester Brown. "Our agriculture existence has evolved over the last 11,000-year period of rather remarkable climate stability. There have been a few little blitzes here and there, but basically it has been stable. Now, suddenly, the climate system is beginning to drastically change. Our agriculture as of today is designed to maximize production with the old climate system, and now, suddenly, we are getting an increasing mismatch between the agriculture system and the climate system. This is creating stress to Mother Earth and it is making it much more difficult to expand food production fast enough to keep up with the rise in population growth."

Brown continued, "Normally, for the country as a whole, we would have 40 percent of our corn planted by the beginning of May. This year, I think we had 13 percent in the ground by May. We are way behind. Why is this a problem? Because if the corn is planted too late, yields begin to go down; because the corn plant then pollinates during the intense heat of summer rather than before the highest temperatures come. Corn is very vulnerable to intense heat. You know when you do corn on a cob, you try to get rid of all those silk strands? Those silk strands are part of the corn's reproductive process, and each kernel site on the cob has, in the early stages, silk strands that come out the end of the ear. When pollination occurs from the tassel, the corn plant, and the pollen, falls down. A grain of pollen falls on each of those strands and the silk strand is like a fallopian tube. It is hollow inside, and it carries the pollen to the kernel site fertilized. Then fertilization occurs and you get a kernel of corn. The problem is if it is too hot, and too dry, the corn silk on the outside of the ear turns brown and dries up and pollination does not occur. You get almost a total crop failure with no corn."

Lester continued, "The world grain harvest is just over two billion tons a year. In America we produce 400 million tons of that, or a fifth of the world's food. We are the breadbasket of the world. Far and away, we are the world's largest exporter, so what happens to the US grain crop is of great concern to the world at large. For example, during the Moscow heat wave in the summer of 2010, we saw Russian grain harvest go from close to 100 million tons to 60 million tons. That is a 40 percent reduction. If that heat wave had been centered not in Moscow but in Chicago, the US could have lost 40 percent of a

400 million ton harvest—or 160 million tons. That would have dropped world grain stocks, carry-over stocks, to the lowest level recording ever, and it would have created total chaos in the world grain market.

"What's worse," Lester warns, "is that cropping patterns are changing. Bird migratory patterns are in flux. The whole system is upside down. Maybe the Russians can farm a little farther north now, sure. But let's look at last year's summer, when the average temperature in Moscow for the month of July was fourteen degrees above the norm. The heat wave in Russia went on for weeks and weeks. It started in late June, went through July. By early August, there were three or four hundred new fires starting every day in western Russia. Totally out of control. They couldn't begin to think about it." As Lester was sharing the information, I could sense his frustration with humanity, corporations, governments, everyday individuals, and our collective inability to connect the dots. He continued, "If someone would have told me in early summer that the average temperature in Moscow would be fourteen degrees above the norm for the whole month of July, I would have said—and I'm not a climate denier—that that's beyond the range of any reasonable possibility.

"Look at the climate incident in central Pakistan," offered Brown. "It hit a record temperature of 128 degrees Fahrenheit. This was in late June, when glaciologist Iqbal Khan pointed this out. It translated into heat, so extreme heat that the glaciers in the Himalayas, in the upper regions of the Indus River Basin, were melting much faster than normal, and it was coupled with the onslaught of the seasonal heavy rains. You had already swollen rivers because of the accelerated melting of the glaciers, and then the rainfall came. It escalated the problem. I mean, ice melting is clearly one of the factors, but most people do not link ice melting with Pakistan which has had some of the most severe flooding. In fact, during the worst flooding on record, a fifth of Pakistan was underwater. You can imagine a fifth of the United States being underwater. This was extraordinary. I don't think we've begun to grasp what it is we're doing, and what the consequences will be. "

Brown further explained, "Here in Washington, when you talk about national security with people, automatically they think weapon systems and huge expenditures, but who—I mean who—is going to attack us? We are the United States of America, the largest superpower in the world! What we need to do now, in the early twenty-first century, is sit down with a fresh pad of paper and ask ourselves what are the threats to our security today? Not what were they in the last century. What are they today? Climate change, spreading water shortages, collapsing fisheries, shrinking forests, eroding soils, failing states. When you look at our current realities, armed aggression doesn't even make the top five on my threats to security. It may or may not even make the top 10."

Politics, inertia, and bureaucracy! That's our government. That's most governments around the world. I needed to start to think outside the box if I was going to find a way to tackle any of this. As I continued my climate change investigation on Capitol Hill, I met up with author Andrew Winston over at the Jefferson Memorial to discuss the latest developments he writes about in his new book *Green to Gold*. Andrew began discussing our collective unconsciousness. "We walk into our house, turn on the lights. We don't really care that 50 percent came from coal, and that burning coal is frying the planet or causing degeneration of our air quality. It's not just, you know, that we're clueless. I mean, when you look at a sort of psychological assessment of what are the kinds of things that we as people have trouble getting worked up about, climate change fits the bill perfectly as the kind of thing you can't get going about because it's diffused. You can't see it, it's broad, it's across the whole planet; it doesn't hit you specifically, you know? It's everything that makes it hard for us to work on. That's why it's so challenging.

"Climate change effects are harder to grasp," he explained. "I mean, because we think of it as someone else's storm. Even the scientists say 'so and so's storm.' You can't say what's climate change. We do ourselves a disservice when we do those kinds of disclaimers that are technically accurate, but sort of missed the mark—it's like impressionism. It's like, yeah, this one dot doesn't make that picture, but if you step back, the drought in Russia, the floods in Pakistan, the floods in Australia, the floods in Nashville, this is climate change. This is what it looks like. What we can't say for sure is how often that will happen or, you know, to where exactly, but this is what it looks like.

"And it should be scaring us enough to call to action the way World War II was a global call to action. It doesn't seem to though, and it's one of the biggest questions of our time. Why can't we mobilize for this? We mobilize when there's economic interest. We can see there's economic interest. But the interests making money on fossil fuels are focused on their income, and the interests that could make money fighting climate change are not. Not in America. We're competing now for this new clean economy, and China, Germany, and others are leading the pack."

Andrew definitely stirred my brain. Where is America headed? Are we still operating in Neanderthal times, building our war chest, preparing for battle, or will we evolve to a new consciousness, one based on an American spirit of renewables, one that's clean, fresh, and innovative?

"I think we're having sort of an existential kind of crisis in this country about what we're about," adds Andrew. "I think we've got some very divisive forces that are very dangerous, and we don't seem to know how to effectively fight or deal with them. Unfortunately, right now, when it comes to climate change, we're seeing very little of the unexpected in our political system. Nobody really says anything that's against the party line anymore, and I don't know how we're gonna get through these tough times. This is what makes me nervous about our country. The political system is broken."

It was time for action. I could see our political system was in gridlock. I knew I needed to act differently in my approach. Healing the planet was going to take the creation of a new consciousness.

When I first met up with William McDonough, founder and principal of William McDonough + Partners, Architects and

Community Designers, I was intrigued by the detail in which he had developed his strategy to tackle problems. He was co-founder of McDonough Braungart Design Chemistry, with Michael Braungart, and also co-founder of the Cradle to Cradle Products Innovation Institute in San Francisco.

"Cradle to Cradle grew out of a synaptic space that was created by me and Michael Braungart in our first meeting," said William McDonough, by way of introduction. "I had been involved as an architect in the Green Movement. In fact, we did the first green office building for the Environmental Defense Fund in New York in 1984. Then I met some people while working on a design of a daycare center in Germany, and I won a competition there. I was looking at the children in the daycare center. Toddlers. They were chewing on everything, and I said, I need an eco-toxicologist to check this place out, because I don't know what it is they're chewing."

"A what?" I asked.

He replied, "An eco-toxicologist. What's an eco-toxicologist? Someone who understands the toxicology of your environment. I was looking for someone who could accurately have access to the science of what it was we were surrounding ourselves with. I looked for that for years, and then I found one in New York when Dr. Michael Braungart arrived from Germany. He'd been the head of Greenpeace's chemistry section. He was the most famous person in the universe I was searching for." I smiled as McDonough shared his insight into his union with Michael, as I had been in touch with him myself over the past year.

"Well, you see," began McDonough, "the reason Michael and I are so close, and so intensely connected, is when we talk to each other, we share ideas. It's all based on a fundamental premise that we're here to celebrate a world of abundance and joy and love. We are not bound by our limits and concerns, or about a sort of rare sense of the world, or a sense of greed. We're not here to be less bad; we're here to be more good, and a lot of people think that being less bad is being good, but it's not because it's not mathematics. This is not: two negatives are equal to one point of a positive. Less is a relationship between two things; bad is a human value we impose. A tool has no value except for the purposes to which it has been put. That is human intention.

"What Michael brings with his science in chemistry and toxicology is clarity and truth from a scientific perspective. What I bring as a designer is intentionality. When you put those two together, you get what we call design chemistry—the foundation principles of Cradle to Cradle. The notion is, 'How do we love all the children of all species for all time?' That's our value setup, and we've found that to be incredibly useful for design, because nature supports growth. The idea is the world gets better. That's design. Steve Jobs said that when asked about the iPod. He said, 'In the end, the job of design is to make the world better. That's what we do.' The idea of nature design is quite astonishing, really. We look for a condition of support where one species supports another species. Birds support biota falling to the forest floor in the rainforest, and everything is in symbiosis. We exist in the synaptic space where the idea is that things get better, more functant and richer. That when you return to nature, follow nature's rules, everything gets better.

"Michael had developed something called the intelligent product system," explained McDonough. "The idea was to see things as either biological nutrients or technical nutrients. In other words, things should be characterized as either going back to the soil, in which case, they have to be totally safe in the biosphere and certainly, yes, humans and things like that. If lead gets into the biosphere, for instance, it's a neurotoxin, so that's not appropriate biological material because it's toxifying. On the other hand, in a technical nutrient, such as a camera or computer, lead may not be exposed to people because of the cases and what not, and if that computer went back to the computer industry without being released into the biosphere, lead would be contained in a technosphere where it can be safely handled and return to human utility in the U-cycle. We see materials as either going back to nature, or going back to industry if they are contaminated, but still useful."

William expanded, "I started creating a protocol where we would, if looking for materials, we would always ask a forest what it wanted to give us, instead of telling it what we wanted. We wouldn't necessarily specify a certain species, because if you look at the word 'mahogany,' that's all you know how to ask for, then you deforest the place in search of 'mahogany.' But if you go into the forest and say, 'What woods do you have?' then we may have woods we've never seen before, and they're incredibly beautiful. They all have these different characteristics, allowing the forest to maintain its full species. And so, we value every tree for its qualities, and you end up with a delightfully diverse palette of beautiful things that support the local people. You also end up with a forest that can regenerate with the same genome.

"It's more like we revel in its creativity and its fecundity," added McDonough. "As human designers, we need to be extremely humble because it took us 5,000 years to put wheels on our luggage. We're not very smart, you know. So I look at a tree for design inspiration, and I say, 'What's the design of a tree?' The tree answers, 'Build me a home that makes oxygen, sequesters carbon, can fix nitrogen, distill water, provide habitat for hundreds of species, accrue solar energy as fuel, make complex sugar into food, build soil, create microclimates, change colors and self-replicate.' How many human buildings have made oxygen lately? Nature is an incredibly sophisticated designer."

William was a genius. My overall impression was that he was open to share and could sense I was in a state of deep appreciation, amazed at his brilliant capacity of taking complex subjects and bringing them down into simple layman terms. I got it. Nature had the blueprint. We just had to follow it.

He continued, "Are you aware of the Hannover Principles?"

"The Hannover Principles?" I replied. "What are they?"

"The Hannover Principles of Sustainable Design," William began, gently, "are nine principles that we prepared in New York when I was there from 1991–92. We were working with Michael in Hannover at the time. They were the design guidelines for sustainability for the World's Fair for the year 2000. They were gifted from Hannover to the Earth Summit. I wrote them very carefully with our team, and they've held up ever since then. We defined, for ourselves, the principles of sustainable design in 1991, and it grew out of work we'd been doing."

McDonough continued, "The first one is to allow nature and humans to coexist in peace and harmony, and include things like eliminating the concept of waste. We don't ask for zero waste, because one must exist. We say, eliminate the concept of waste. You see, all these materials have nutrients and it flows in cycles. Cherry trees using a nutrient to create a blossom. Then the blossom goes back to the soil, and so it's not about closed loops. It's really about how things get used for a period of time, and then they go back to the fecund system—that is the planet. We're not taking things back 500 miles to where they were produced. That creates waste. We're taking things, used things, used utilities, and putting them in the world in a way that allows us to put out continuous nutrients for all to benefit from.

"We need builders to begin to focus on the concept of design for abundance," explained McDonough, adding, "The idea that there is abundant solar energy; imagine if it was the only income on the planet. There is an abundance of water, if we know how to manage it in a way that is delightfully effective. We know ways to clean it. I mean, we can take the humble water pump at the Hudson Valley and put water in it and leave it in the sun for twelve hours (two days, six hours a day) and it will kill—with ultraviolet light from the sunshine—every living thing in that bottle, including cholera. Abundant, helpful, solar energy.

"We've also discovered you can't innovate while bench-marking. True innovation happens outside of benchmarking," continued McDonough. "Google never benchmarked becoming Encyclopedia Britannica as a goal. They didn't get up and go 'Oh, we have twice as many references as the Encyclopedia Britannica.' Who cares? They innovate from different places. Old thinking doesn't work, the red ocean of competition isn't a useful model. It's a series of new metrics, it's the blue ocean of the joy of creativity."

William and I talked for a few more hours. He'd explain a concept, and I'd ask a flurry of questions. He'd define an idea, and my mind swirled with the possibilities. The conversation should be about what we can do. Not about what we haven't been able to do. And listening to the earth was the key. When we concluded, he gave me a hug and wished me well on my journey.

Over the course of the next few weeks, my thoughts were haunted from all the information that William McDonough had shared with me. I was looking for a way to process everything and put some of it into action when my friend Tara Sheahan called me out of the blue, asking me to meet her wisdom teacher, Ananda Giri, who was visiting from India. He was in town and she thought he could be very helpful in assisting me in completing my peace journey. I was curious what she meant by that. Ananda Giri was with a spiritual organization called One World Academy whose sole purpose is life education. When I asked, Tara told me simply, "Greg, One World

Academy's mission is to help us move from a place of conflict to joy." Sounded right up my alley.

Ananda was super slim, dressed in white pants and a light blue sweatshirt. He was quiet and stood for a while by himself, looking over the Malibu coastline, when I first arrived. We began our journey walking down the hill toward the meadow. I shared with Ananda my spiritual journey and my backstory at UMASS Amherst, my trauma I experienced during the First Gulf War, and my inspiration to heal the earth by planting trees. I sort of just gushed it all out, but it somehow seemed exactly the way it was supposed to happen. Ananda's interest was piqued, and he started talking about my passion: trees.

"Trees," Ananda began. "We think trees are not part of our body ... not a part of us. Can you separate yourself from this tree? If the tree exists, you exist. If the tree perishes, you perish. These lungs supply oxygen to all parts of my body. Where do the lungs get their oxygen? From the trees that surround us. Then, is it not true that the tree is an extended part of our body? It's just another organ, one that's not sitting inside this body. Truly caring for yourself means caring for the world that surrounds you. Caring for this tree, caring for this planet. We are all connected. The question is: To what degree do we realize our connectedness?"

Here was a man stating as fact what I'd always believed, but thought I was alone in believing. My connection to trees was not my own. It was all of us, connected. "The very idea that we are separate individuals," continued Ananda, "I think it's a very erroneous perception. How could you be separate from the others? Many of us talk about how we're all connected in spirit, but is it true that we're just connected in spirit? Even physically, we are inseparable. Is there something that we can think of in our lives, one moment in our lives we can proclaim and see, that is not dependent on anything else? No. Ridiculous. Every single moment is dependent on another moment, and that other moment is dependent on so many other moments. We are connected. It is not a question of whether or not we must become connected. It's a question of, 'Do we realize our connectedness and do we learn to live and function from this perception of connectedness?'

"Let us talk of this moment," Ananda continued. "This moment, you are sitting on this lovely Southern California cliff in Malibu, you're filming me, and more than filming, you're working to make a difference to this world. That's the reason we're having this dialogue. We're trying to learn from each other, and I'm sure there'll be hundreds, maybe thousands, maybe millions benefitting from this project. This moment, this point in time, this dialogue, this vision of yours, will translate into thousands and millions being affected. Do we know how many people are involved in this project? Do we know how many ideas have gone into this project? Do we know how much technology has gone into this project? How many inventions have gone into this project? This moment could not exist without you, without me, without this amazing crew around us, without these lovely Malibu Hills, without this lovely weather. This moment could not exist without the camera with which you shoot. This moment could not exist without the microphones everywhere. This moment would not exist without the information technology that's available in this world, without the internet. Maybe this moment would not exist if the Wright Brothers didn't invent the flying machine. Into this single moment, literally the whole of human civilization has gone into this moment. Can you separate the Wright Brothers from this moment? Can we separate the man who made this camera from this moment? Can you separate yourself from this moment? Can we separate these hills from this moment? Not just human civilization, it's literally the whole universe that has gone into this moment. When do you realize this?

"If you can bring attention to this moment, examine this moment, and ask a question, a simple question, does this moment exist on its own, or is this moment dependent on many factors?" asked Ananda. "These many factors include many people, many ideas, and the whole of creation itself. This is true for any other moment in life for that matter. You're hungry. You go to the restaurant. You order a sandwich, and put that sandwich into your mouth. You feel so happy. That one moment, when you grab the sandwich, you eat that sandwich, and then you feel so satisfied that you're full. Do you know how much has gone into that moment?

"Somebody had to create that restaurant. Somebody had to make that sandwich. Somebody had to grab tomatoes in Southern California, and maybe you had to import cheese, mozzarella from Italy. Somebody had to milk the cows or buffalos and make cheese out of it, and somebody had to fly across the Atlantic to California with that cheese. Somebody had to drive a truck from some place to some place, so that you get to fill your stomach. If you brought attention to that moment, you would see how many people are involved. How much has gone into it, not just people, as I mentioned earlier, again, for you to enjoy the sandwich with the tomato, for the tomato to really grow, it needed sun, it needed the soil, it needed the farmers, it needed the fertilizers. In every moment of ours, every single experience of ours, literally, the whole of human civilization, the whole world, the whole planet is involved. Even physically, we are connected, not just in our spirits.

"You look at yourself and ask the questions, 'Who am I?' or 'Who are you?' You are a result, an experience of x number of factors, and those factors being the number of ideas that have gone into you, your parents of course, your friends, and all the vegetables you've consumed, all the fruits you've consumed, all the milk you've consumed, all the meat you've consumed." Ananda took in a deep breath, as if to take in the totality of the universe in that breath. As if he was breathing in all of mankind.

When he began again, it seemed to be from a super peaceful place. "In other words, if you looked at your body, there is the fish in you. There is the cow in you, the plants, the trees. And the plant has become you. The trees have become you. Your friends have become you. These ideas have become you. Even at the broad physical level, are you separate from the other? The answer is no. And if we are really looking for a conflict-free world, we believe at the One World Academy it's of utmost significance that there's a shift in our perception. Right now we're so rooted in the idea that 'I'm separate from the others.' As long as we live and function from this belief, it can only create conflict. As long as you perceive yourself to be a separate individual, you cannot but look for your survival. All that will matter to you is only yourself, your significance, and everything you do will exemplify this. It's only when we move from this perception to a new perception that we are connected and function from that new perception. Only then can we be expected to live in peace and harmony and leave behind the conflict world. And for this to happen, it requires attention, awareness."

Wow! That crazy idea I had thirty years ago of planting trees and saving the world didn't seem so farfetched anymore. Ananda had woken the inner child in me. Why did trees speak to me? I was looking for my connection to the trees. This conversation was so intense. I wasn't connected to the trees. I *was* the trees. *We* are the trees. But if we come from the forests, and we are all interconnected, then what's our higher purpose? Do we have one?

The Great Wake-Up Call

We but mirror the world. All the tendencies present in the outer world are to be found in the world of our body. If we could change ourselves, the tendencies in the world would also change. As a man changes his own nature, so does the attitude of the world change towards him. This is the divine mystery supreme. A wonderful thing it is, and the source of our happiness. We need not wait to see what others do.

—MAHATMA GANDHI

When you turn on the weather channel, there's this montage of images of storms, superstorms, earthly disasters, flooding, lightning, and displacement. Do we ever think how one storm, one fallen tree, or one dying coral reef affects the entirety of our living planet, and if not, what's it going to take to wake up? Is time running out? Are disasters multiplying, and, if so, what can any one of us do about it?

Again, Deepak Chopra's words came to me as the voice of reason. "Paradigm shifts do not happen overnight," he explained, "and yet they seem to happen overnight. It's like a fruit that takes a long time to ripen, and then it falls suddenly. But it falls when it's ripe. So, too, do shifts in collective consciousness take a long time to ripen. But when they reach a critical mass: then suddenly the shift is there."

Avon Mattison, a peace building consultant who has worked with the United Nations Economic and Social Council as an official Peace Messenger, is the originator of Creative/Integrative Decision-Making, a process she began in 1961. Her process, when applied to corporate, institutional, and governmental life, funnels decisions made by those structures through the paradigm of how each step taken can further our goal of a peaceful world of coexistence. A world where children of this and future generations live in peace interculturally. She's also the founder of the International Day of Peace, which we celebrate each year on September 21. "We live in a war culture," she began. "A culture of peace begins with every thought, word, and action every human being takes every moment of every day. It's a decision each one of us makes every moment. Our thoughts, words, and actions affect not only ourselves but have a radiating effect in everyone in our lives." I'd heard her words before, and had celebrated the International Day of Peace, but only now was I starting to understand the profound changes my own thoughts had on the rest of the world.

I met up with author and thought leader Marc Barasch back in the woods of Los Angeles to discuss this idea of each of us being part of a whole. Marc is the author of *The Compassionate Life* and founder of the Green World Campaign. Marc thought the woods would be an ideal location for us to walk and talk, to be among the trees.

"We imagine ourselves to be separate," Barasch began. "We suffer from what Einstein called 'the optical delusion of consciousness,' that we're individuals and we're not connected to the whole of nature. Trees are not only a symbol that exist deep in the human psyche but is at the center of every narrative of every faith tradition. They're also called the Swiss army knife of nature. They do everything. They can bring back aquifers, moisturize micro-climates, provide food, fodder, fuel, building materials, help crops, and of course, remove CO_2 from the atmosphere. It's the reason that the trees have always been venerated spiritually as well as pragmatically.

"We also share our DNA with trees," Marc continued. "The tree mimics the human body. It has feet, a trunk, and limbs. It bears fruit. It has seeds."

I had never even imagined there was a link between the DNA of a tree and our DNA, but of course there is. Was nature trying to teach us something? Giving us a model to work from?

Marc continued, "When we look at an aspen grove, it looks like a collection of individuals, but actually underneath the grove is a single organism where the entire root system is connected.

Trees symbolize the solitary of individuals growing strong vertically. But there is also this sort of underground dimension to an aspen grove whereby the root systems link together. It's actually entwined to the point that, under the surface, an aspen grove is a single organism. This appearance of separateness and the reality of interconnectedness is the metaphor we seek. An aspen grove supplies us with so much we can quantify above the surface, but it really expresses our existential condition together. We're. Not. Separate.

"The complexity of our understanding of the forests is rudimentary to our understanding of ourselves," continued Marc, "because, it is really our sense of identity that is screwing things up in the world. We have this individual identity, king or queen mentality of the world that it belongs to us. On the contrary, agroforestry really is about a co-created relationship between humanity and nature. I mean we got this idea from environmentalism, as a movement, that we're somehow the depredating hand of existence. We always ruin things. We think of nature as something we have to, sort of, fence off and protect from ourselves. That we are the problem. That we are the users. That we are the plunderers.

"Whereas if you go back in prehistory, when we study our past, there has always been this incredibly synergistic relationship between what human beings were doing, how they fostered nations, and how they were genuinely stewards of the garden. They got their needs met while also regenerating nature on a constant basis. That's the beauty of what I call 'regenerative ecology.' Ecological Regeneration is restoring land and restoring community. It's about how we live in harmony with nature. The idea of green compassion, for me, is a real universal concern. We have universal responsibilities. The Dalai Lama says, 'How do we create a civilization of life?' To me, it's not really a moral issue, but rather it's really the nature of things. The natural state we should be existing in. A state of compassion. Green compassion. And compassion really means that we're connected to everybody and all living beings at all times, in all places forever.

"What is our actual purpose as a civilization?" Marc asked as he picked up a leaf that had fallen from one of the surrounding trees, tracing its parallel veins. "I think we can begin to reformulate society by starting with our own lives, with the heart itself, and the emotional content of how we feel about nature. Can we change the paradigm with love? If love isn't the central organizing principle, if compassion isn't the organizing principle of civic life, and therefore our lives with each other and with the natural world, we're not going to make it. We can't just do it by rational calculus. We have to be a civilization of love. This heartfulness is not ornamental. It's not secondary. It's not just a nice set of doilies, hearts, and flowers sort of thing. It's fundamental to how we relate, and how we understand ourselves to be—in a web of relationships. Every time one strand of that web twitches, the entire web shutters. Even a small fold, even a small action, affects everything. We just never know what's going to ripple out and have this larger effect."

The idea that my actions were like a momentary plink on the web of humanity was fascinating. I knew that this journey I was on was changing me, changing my thought patterns, and that I was evolving. What I had not thought about was that my journey might be changing the world, changing everything... that it could reverberate out across the web. Were the steps I was taking today toward understanding my connectiveness part of someone else's journey? Were their steps pushing me forward, to learn, to expand my understanding of the nature of peace itself? I could feel the world evolving with me. It was as if peace was a bud blooming.

"That's because global consciousness is hearing the wake-up call," said environmentalist and activist Paul Hawken when I shared the results of my recent work. Paul's book *Drawdown: The Most Comprehensive Plan Ever Proposed to Reverse Global Warming* is just that, a call to action. "Relationships between humans and living systems are coming to an extraordinary point of crisis," says Paul, "and this point of crisis is underlined by this growing human awareness. This strange way in which the world is organizing itself—it's not just transnational. It's transcultural; it's almost beyond time. Something is arising. There's something deeper happening here. What we're seeing is humanity's immune response. There's something happening in civilization that's like a living system. We're collectively manifesting intelligence. Life creates the conditions that are conducive to life. That's what we're all here to do. That's the wonderful thing about nature. It's always balanced. There's no such thing as imbalance. Life creates life."

I returned home. Meditating. Breathing. A new sense of awareness was unfolding. I finished my Transcendental Meditation and received another call from Tara Sheahan. She was like stardust sprinkling a little consciousness on me with her magic wand of energy, ensuring I was in the moment. She wanted me to catch up with her husband, Casey Sheahan, the CEO at Patagonia. Casey was an avid fisherman and a true family man. When I arrived at his offices, I saw the pictures of his two boys on his desk. He was wearing his traditional Patagonia sweatshirt, was happy to see me, and told me he could recognize my progress. He could tell I had lost weight and was radiating a different sort of glow, giving off a feeling of centered calm. "When I think about roots, I also think about the planet itself," Casey began. "Its desire to create seeds to propagate. Those seeds are the future. And those seeds carry a different twist genetically than the roots and plants that they come from. They allow for change, because nature is about change."

In the weeks that followed, I made plans to head down to Costa Rica in an effort to meet with José María Figueres, Costa Rica's former president, who is still involved in causes to mitigate climate change, encourage sustainable development, and develop emerging technology to support those ideals. It was a journey in itself—traveling to Central America, finding him, setting up the meeting. The country still has so many untouched parts it sometimes feels prehistoric. It is definitely one of those spots on earth where you feel more connected to nature.

José was eager to discuss his efforts, and began by explaining a little about the history of his country. "The abolition of the army," he explained, "allowed our country to generate a 'peace dividend.' Over the years, we have successfully invested in health and well-being, education, infrastructure, and everything that makes people live better within a society. Our country is also committed to preserving our 5 percent share of the world's total biodiversity. Creating a carbon tax is part of that work. With the proceeds of our carbon tax, Costa Rica has had the resources to pay for environmental services. Small farmers, who previously could grow only rice, are now moving into planting trees."

The Costa Rican experience was the embodiment of my search—a country that is nonviolent, has no army, is self-reflective, integrated, eco-minded, healthful, and aware of our interconnectedness. Who would have ever imagined that a peace dividend would be derived from nature; that allowing biodiversity to thrive also serves as a mirror for our own well-being? It was a long path this tiny country took to transform itself into a peace state. But they did it; they sowed the seeds of peace, and they reaped the benefits.

I was awakened. I had found a new purpose. New intention. I returned home, threw my bags in the house, and got in my car...heading down the Pacific Coast Highway. I wanted to return to my favorite place in the Palisades: The Self-Realization Fellowship Lake Shrine. As I stood over their sacred lake, I thought of all the great wisdom teachers whom I met, who shared their sage circumspection, and helped me along my journey. Each of these individuals had helped me grow and evolve my consciousness, fully nurturing my soul being.

I watched the dragonflies skip the water and thought about the words of Lama Surya Das in his book *Awakening the Buddha Within: Eight Steps to Enlightenment—Tibetan Wisdom for the Western World*. It's all about the eight steps to enlightenment, the path that Buddha took, and speaks of how to become a Buddha one-self, how anybody can be awakened—awakened from the sleep of delusion and confusion and misunderstanding, where the causes of happiness, fulfillment, and love really lie.

"Awakening," says Surya Das, "means to see things as they are, not as they ain't; to become more than we are and can be, to find ourselves, self-realization, inner and external illumination, clear-seeing, open heart, awakened mind, this kind of thing. It's the fullest flowering of our capacities to really recognize who and why we are. Because we're all, as we say in Tibetan, we're all Buddhas, not Buddhists, God forbid. We're all Buddhas by nature. It's only momentary obscurations that veil that fact, like the sun behind the clothes of our obscuring and conflicting emotions and passions. The Buddha, the true Buddha, is innate awareness. Newness. Awareness itself. And this is very important to recognize in all the images as it just mirrors our highest, deepest, best Buddha-like self. We say, if you want peace in the world, you have to become peace to make peace, so we try to root out the roots of violence and anger in our hearts; that there is no way to peace. Peace itself is the way."

Standing beside the ashes of Gandhi, lovingly enshrined at the Fellowship, reminded me of my journey and commitment to mankind finding peace, for all of us to "be the change we want to see in the world." I found a spot and took the time to reflect on my journey. As I was completing my meditation, I slowly opened my eyes to be greeted by Brother Achalananda, one of the gate-keeper and spiritual teachers of Self Realization Fellowship.

He began, "Do you know why my spiritual name is Brother Achalananda? Since we are a member of the Ancient Order of Sannyassis, we also have a last name, which represents one of the ten branches of the ancient swami order. Paramahansa Yogananda, my guru, belonged to the Giri (Hill) Order or branch. And so Achalananda, A-C-H-A-L-A-N-A-N-D-A, is a compound word formed of Achala, which literally means steady mountain or not moving. The not moving aspect of that has many different meanings; permanent, unchanging, undiminished, and so forth, and Ananda, which means bliss, so the name means mountain of bliss or permanent bliss. Not too bad a name."

As I write this, I smile remembering Achalananda Giri sharing. Had I reached the mountain of bliss? Could I? Perhaps it's the simple things in life that bring forth our greatest peace. As we sat together on a perfect day in dappled sunlight, he reminded me, "If you're really looking for a breakthrough, you must inquire into yourself. You must examine the condition that caused you conflict. You must examine the conditions that caused you sorrow. You must look inside yourself and find the root cause of that conflict and sorrow. Then you'll have a breakthrough. If the world must transform, the individual must transform. You are the world. You cannot separate yourself from the world. Individual transformation is global transformation."

Brother Achalananda rose and walked with me around the pond. We reflected on Gandhi and who he is and what he represents. "When I mention his name, what resonates with you?" Brother Achalananda asked.

"Well, I think that he was a person who lived his beliefs very powerfully and had very high and noble ideas of a certain belief and about gaining India's freedom through peaceful means."

"Yes," Brother Achalananda responded. "And in that, he had to train the people of India to be what he calls Satyagrahas, insisters of truth; so that they could seek to free India by nonviolent means through speaking truth."

"Well, Gandhi had the brains and spiritual understanding enough to realize that the end is the product of the means," I offered. "So, whenever they would lose as a result of using violent means, killing and retaliating, he wouldn't meet with them anymore. He'd just go back and start fasting and praying until they said, 'Come back, lead us, we need you.'"

"He believed in certain things very powerfully and he wrote about it in his autobiography," Brother Achalananda explained. "In his book *My Experiments with Truth,* Gandhi very powerfully states that 'truth is God.' Mind you, truth is God, not God is truth … truth is God, showing that which comes out of God, that which is truthful and factual, that's the real thing. He was a political saint. You don't see too many politicians that are saints, but he certainly showed his sainthood in his own life."

"And yet," I interjected, "at the same time, he was practical. He had an understanding as an individual, being in the Indian army. He understood the hurt of war, and sometimes the need for it, from when he was offshore in the Indian army, in Western India, right? As I understand it, certainly by the 1930s, Gandhi's followers knew his concept of ahimsa and were familiar with his practice of nonviolence, and they went to him (some of the high officers in the army) and they asked him 'Well, what should we do if the country is attacked?' He said, 'You defend it. You defend your country.'"

"These people were soldiers, right? Their job was to defend their nation," explained Brother Achalananda. "Gandhi was telling them, 'Do your job.' But the thing is, you have three ways you can deal with violence coming from other people. You can deal with it nonviolently, but still resist it and say 'Hey, I won't go along with what you're doing. If you're going to do it, you're going to have to go over my dead body' and they very well may do that. Or you can say, 'Yes, I forgive you' and run away. That's a coward approach. That's not right. Or you can defend it violently if you have to. If what you feel is absolutely and exclusively a matter of wanting to protect innocent people, then it is all right. He was telling his soldiers, 'I understand.' The thing is to not have hatred while using violence to defend others, and that's not easy. The real deep meaning of ahisma, according to our paramguru, Swami Sri Yukteswar Giri, is the removal of the desire to kill. He said, 'This world is inconveniently arranged for a literal practice of ahisma.' If you overcome the desire to kill, then you'll do everything possible not to kill. But you have to overcome that desire, and that's the first step.

"This is part of our spiritual evolution," continued Brother Achalananda. "The ancient sage Patanjali, in his yoga sutras, lays out the eight limbs, or eight steps, we must take for understanding the source from where we came and where we must return, and ultimately for attaining direct perception of truth. The first two of those steps are called 'yama' and 'niyama.' Yama literally means control, so these are the restraints—things that you do not do. There are five of them. There are also five moral observances, which are niyama. These are the positive things you do and are very similar to the ten commandments of Moses. The very first yama is ahimsa: the principle of nonviolence toward all living things. You should restrain your violent nature. This is the very first thing you should refrain from, first in the ten commandments, first in yama. But even being nonviolent… well, that's a pretty big step to take.

"These ten yama and niyamas are 'the great vow' in India, and other religions and cultures try to follow these principles as well. This is a great vow to commit to and to guide your life, but if you can do this, it puts your life on a strong moral foundation, because these are basically moral phenomena," continued Brother Achalananda. "You don't kill, you don't steal, you don't lie, and you have to have the proper attitude about what our teachers would call 'continence' or self-restraint. So, you have these kinds of things from which you abstain, or deal with in a proper way, and as you begin to work with each one of them, you will realize they are all somewhat interconnected. As you begin to deal with life through this way of being, you then begin to experience the deeper meanings behind the observance of the yamas and niyamas.

"Now, interestingly, the things you should do of the niyama: the very first one is shaucha, which literally means purity or cleanliness," continued Brother Achalananda. "Here you're talking about purity of the mind and also purity, or cleanliness, of the body. If you want to try to live a spiritual life, you have to get your thoughts in order. You have to learn how to behave, in other words. These are things that you must do, up to the very last one, the last niyama: surrender to God. This is a very interesting one because in surrendering to God, we don't want to just say, 'Okay, this is happening, I don't like it, it is not my will, but thy will be done.' But when you submit your life in harmony with what God wants, then that is the positive aspect of this principle. You basically are working in a positive way toward attuning your life to God, so that you will be receptive to what God wants.

"Then there's santosha, which is contentment," continued Brother Achalananda. "Contentment is no small thing. It means you are perfectly content with whatever comes your way. You deal with it in a peaceful manner. You're basically a happy individual. You're content. Nothing can shake you. Well, what the world has to learn is that you don't achieve contentment by what you have. You'll achieve contentment by what you are. There are people with everything, and they are miserable people. They're not contented people. They're unhappy people. Despite having all material, success, and wealth, that won't necessarily bring happiness in your life. You have to develop a peaceful character. You have to develop this thing called inner peace.

"Self-realization," continued Brother Achalananda, "well, sometimes people misunderstand that term because they think of the 'self' in terms of ego. They think it is a way to realize your ego. We don't have to realize our ego. We're very familiar with it all the time. 'Self,' with a capital S, really means soul. What we do have to recognize and get in contact with is our soul. Ego is nothing but soul attached to a form. Because it's inhabiting that form, soul is the silent witness of what is going on."

At this, Brother Achalananda paused our walk, taking a moment to feel the sun. He seemed to be listening to a voice I didn't hear. Then he began to walk again, and continued, "As a human being, we have free choice. We always have free choice. We can do whatever we want. You can say, 'I'll do this' or 'I won't do that,' and so we have a lot of freedom, but with that freedom comes responsibility and if we don't make good choices, then we create what is called bad karma. Karma is nothing but the law of cause and effect, that as you sow, so shall you reap. As one person jokingly said, 'A lot of people sow their wild oats for six days a week and then they go to church, or synagogue, etcetera, on Sunday and pray for relief from a crop failure. A lot of us don't want to accept responsibility for our actions. That's something we have to learn to do—character development. Responsibility. When Yogananda found his guru, he was told to surround himself with a spiritual bodyguard and he was reminded all the time, 'Learn to behave.' It was another way of saying you have to behave in a way where your behavior becomes perfect. As Christ said, 'Be ye therefore perfect, as your father in heaven is perfect,' and that's really the goal for all of us.

"Most of us are not making an effort to connect with God, that's the other part," explained Brother Achalananda. "We have to go after God. We have to bring God into our lives. If you want to be at peace, you need God in your life, because that is how you gain peace, by meditation, deep meditation, deep prayer. You have to connect with God because God is peace, God is love,

God is all of these things, and the more we can connect with him, then that begins to rub off on us, right?

"Of course, our environment is stronger than willpower. If you go out and deal with a bunch of worldly people, you're going to tend to become worldly. It is natural. It's stronger than your willpower. But if you strive to find that inner peace, that inner joy that is even beyond that peace of God's presence, that bliss that the saints call the bliss of God, you think that's not going to have an effect on you? You will become more peaceful. You will become calmer. You will become more understanding of others. You will become more thoughtful of others, more compassionate, and that is what it is really all about.

"We should all act in a more spiritual or godly way. That's the way we are supposed to act on this planet. God put us here, but he doesn't come down in this world to intervene all the time. He basically set into law to do unto others as you would do unto you so that if you break the laws, then suffering comes. Suffering is a reminder of how we should behave. It is God's way of saying, 'No, that's not the way you should act. Get your life together.' And so, chaos just comes as a reminder to us. If you begin to understand this and try to make an effort to find your bliss, you'll experience it. You say, 'Oh, if I meditate more, I feel better. I can enjoy people more, I can enjoy my work more.' Why? Because we're not so caught up in that ego which worries about fear. You can be more natural. You can be yourself."

I had certainly found peace in my meditations. I had certainly experienced bliss, both with Britta and in myself, whenever I'd taken the time to breathe, to live in truth, to sow spiritual seeds in myself. Was I finding God within myself? Was the realization of my connectedness to all things part of this bliss? What did living in truth have to do with peace? Was truth the answer?

"Truth is not the product of any one person or any one rule," continued Brother Achalananda. "Truth belongs to everybody and different people connect with it differently. They may express it in different ways, depending on their culture, and the particular people they're dealing with. There will be those outward differences, and you should never expect that to change. There will always be those kinds of differences, differences we can celebrate. But we can all have the same goals. We're all trying to get to the top of the mountain. We're trying to get to that same goal—contact with God, God realization—whether we realize it or not.

"Once you understand this, that we are all on the same path, it doesn't matter how you get up there, which routes you take. Some are long or hard, and others may seem easy. The style of your path doesn't matter. Once you get there, you'll have the same view. When there is a lack of understanding of the different routes to get to the same goal, it can cause problems as we see in the world today. One of the beautiful things about Yogananda is that he emphasized that we are all seeking the same goal—to find God—and thus united our kinship in him. He believed in ecumenicalism before the word was even around or was even being talked about by people. He tried to always bring people together, that's why he called his church the Church of All Religions. Not that we're going to teach every single thing a religion teaches, but he teaches that we are all together, working toward the same goal. Paramahansa Yogananda often referred to the 'highway to the infinite.' He said that regardless of what religious path or set of beliefs one follows, the final ascension from body consciousness to Spirit is the same for everyone. Eventually, we all have to take the same highway, and that is the highway of the spine. You have to get your consciousness in the spine and take it up the spine, because that's how you make that contact with God.

Brother Achalananda continued, "Buddha expresses it very beautifully: 'He who has cows, has care of cows.' The more material things we have, the more worries we have in taking care of them, right? So that was what Paramahansa said, 'Learn to live more simply.' It doesn't mean that you're not happy. You can be very happy if you learn to be simpler."

Something about walking and listening to Brother Achalananda solidified all my discoveries. I found I was filled with joy and ecstasy when it was time to part. I hugged him as we said farewell.

As I looked out over the pond before leaving, I thought of my old Tibetan friend Romio Shrestha who started this journey with me and who, at the time, gave me a crystal ball. Back then, I had no idea what it was and how it was used.

"What is this?" I had asked him.

"It is the most powerful ritual object in Tibetan Buddhism," replied Romio. "It is a tip of a vajra, a ritual object that symbolizes both the properties of a diamond—indestructibility—and a thunderbolt, or irresistible force. This is your thunderbolt.

And for a modern world, to explain what it is, I call it the spiritual Harley Davidson, like the motor bike Harley Davidson." Romio started making the sounds, "Vroom, vroom, same way, you know, from—to go from this consciousness, this illusionary maya consciousness, this world that our mind creates, that seems so real—from that world to go onto a higher dimension, you need one of these. This is like a vehicle, a diamond vehicle. It's known as a diamond vehicle. It helps you find light. It helps you realize you are actually light. Now, have you ever seen a beam of light? True consciousness is like when a river, when a very powerful river, lands in the ocean and loses his name and becomes the ocean. When you realize we actually are all one in different karmic bodies with different purposes, that's consciousness, that's enlightenment. Keep this with you when you meditate. Let it speed you on your way."

CONCLUSION

It's like a baseball game, and it's the seventh inning, and we're down by two runs, but we haven't lost yet. We still have time to turn it around.

—TED TURNER

As much as an inner peace began to take hold of my soul, a sense of urgency and a need to protect all that I now realized was a part of me—the earth, our environment, all of it—began to feel like a ticking clock. I wanted to take the sleeping world by the shoulders and shake it, to tell it to "wake up." That this was the day to change, and that time was of the essence.

The Paley Center for Media, formerly the Museum of Television & Radio, seemed like the perfect place for me to sit down for an interview with the amazing Ted Turner and talk about this sense of urgency I was waking up with every morning. My friends Sally Ranney and Chip Comins, who produce the annual America's Renewable Energy Day event (AREDAY), were kind enough to tell him about the documentary and facilitate a sit-down. Ted tried to reassure me. "It's like a baseball game, and it's the seventh inning," he told me. "We're down by two runs, but we haven't lost yet. We still have time to turn it around."

Martin Luther had been full of hope. Even if he knew that tomorrow the world would go to pieces, he would still plant his apple tree. For me, it was time to find that orchard. It was time to bring together all the pieces of my journey.

The cynical can look at where we are and proclaim our future dead, and I'd certainly come across my share of those with that thinking. Our children, on the other hand, are still full of innocence, wonder, and hope, and so it was there I decided to rekindle my tree journey.

I reached out to the 186th Elementary School of New York with the intention of planting a tree. The classmates had taken to calling themselves "The Peacemakers"—and took up the challenge to look for, live in, and learn ways to succeed. The teachers were referred to as Wise Owl teachers and took a pledge and commitment of working together to make the world a better place by creating peacemakers and not peace breakers. I had read that Principal Marcia Sidney-Reed had said, "If there's no peace, there is no learning." Having kids learn this principle at an early age so it could shape their choices in the future was such a wonderful idea for a learning environment. As I talked with the teachers and students, I was fascinated by their peace-based curriculum. One of the teachers told me, "We talk about peace a lot. There are always two directions you can take: peace making or peace breaking. And I constantly see our students redirecting themselves toward peace making."

It was inspirational to see these youngsters resolving conflict peacefully. I wondered what our forefathers would have thought about these kids when creating our great nation, a nation born of the ashes of war. Was it our beginnings as a nation, one that only happened because a battle was waged, that kept us in this perpetual state of us versus them, of winners versus losers? It was time to look back to take a step forward.

I visited Philadelphia, the city of Brotherly Love, the city in which our Declaration of Independence took form. I stood in front of the liberty building and read these famous words, "We hold these truths to be self-evident, that all men are created equal, that they are endowed by their Creator with certain unalienable Rights, that among them are Life, Liberty, and the pursuit of Happiness." I contemplated what Jefferson, Madison, and our forefathers must have envisioned for our country.

William McDonough had mentioned to me that while attending the University of Virginia he had the privilege of living in the home designed by Thomas Jefferson. Jefferson had written some 33,000 letters and publications in his lifetime, but the one that stood out was our Declaration of Independence, which was written over the course of seventeen days.

"If you were going to figure out what are the basic fundamentals of human rights and come back to tell me with just three things, what would they be?" McDonough asked. "I often imagine life then and what it meant to be alive. I think Jefferson spent a lot of time thinking about that before he put pen to paper."

Jefferson wrote a letter to James Madison in 1789 trying to decide the perfect length of term on a federal bond. To them, one generation was the answer. Jefferson thought it should be nineteen years—it's now thirty years for a federal bond to mature—but his argument was quite amazing. Jefferson said, "The earth belongs to the living."

McDonough explained, "The living…so, what does it mean to be alive, right? The earth belongs to the living. 'No man may by natural right.' You see, this is the time of enlightenment, of discovering that there are natural rights. Now we can talk about the rights of nature as an actual thing. So Jefferson says that no man may, by natural right, own lands or occupy debts greater than those that may be paid during his own lifetime, because if he could, the world would belong to the dead and not to the living. Whoa…so, life. Then liberty and freedom to explore your creative space—amazing. And then the third, pursuit of happiness. Now, if you think about that, that's why that child born in India has to be celebrated for its pursuit of happiness, his or her pursuit of happiness. That's really important, and, unfortunately, I can't imagine the current Congress using the word 'happiness' in a bill so this is a really fundamental document."

William proceeded, "$E = mc^2$, have you ever done that? It's an amazing thing to do. Einstein tricked us. He put the E in the front. If you reversed the formula, it's much easier to do because he put the number at the back. Think about it, $E = mc^2$.

You look for a number, and it's a formula; c is the number, speed of light, and it's 186,000 miles per second. It's one of the largest numbers you can ever amount, even be able to conceive, right? It's almost infinity. Now, square it. So, you're even further out there with a number so large it's almost impossible to make, which means you might as well call it approaching infinity for our purposes. And then the m, the mass; well, that means that if the mass is in any way a positive number, more than nothing, as in one atom, then E is almost infinite. So, one atom is almost infinite energy, the atom bomb."

At that moment, I could see in William's eyes that he had a lot more to share. William continued, "Goodbye Hiroshima. Why was Einstein afraid? What was the intention behind the bomb? This is the real question. It's the value that's in the intention. You realize that if that's the case, then the earth and the sun; nuclear power, are in this relationship. The sun is physics for all intents and purposes; it's a thermonuclear reaction. We are a nuclear-powered planet and our reactor is exactly what we needed ninety-three million miles away and its wireless. What's the big deal? We've got the sun which is the only form of income on the planet. We don't have mass income. The income is from the sun. If we're going to have abundance, we need income. Now that's chemistry, and then what happens? Something amazing occurs. Preserve the quality of the mass; that's one thing, and then we find out that something happens when the sun strikes that heavy amount of gas, which basically Einstein called a mystery. You see, there is no letter in science for what we're dealing with here. It would be B, for it's biology; it's life itself."

It was this moment that my light bulb turned on, and everything for me came full circle. William swelled, "What is life? What is consciousness? What does it mean to be a living thing? What does it mean to be alive? Jefferson had boiled it down to life, liberty, and the pursuit of happiness. His conclusion was based on the concept that to be a living thing you must have one thing: growth. Well, humanity has grown. We're now 7.4 billion people. Let's design our systems to work with those 7.4 billion. If you add up all the ants on earth, they have like 20–30 times the body mass of all humans. Yet they leave no waste, cause no pollution. They're not destroying the planet. Two, you have to have a free form of energy. You have to have income to grow. Where does that come from? The sun; that's it, typically in nature. The third, an open system of chemicals operating for the benefit of the organism's reproduction. It's like open source. All these chemicals have to interact in a way that operates for the benefit of the organism's reproduction. If humans start designing stuff, contrary to that system which is life, well then we have death, so you either have growth or dying. If you're not growing, you're dying."

I was fascinated. Two years ago, I was sitting at this group in Aspen and read this quote about $E = mc^2$, and someone came up and said, "You know, Einstein wrote the theory. And he said, 'No problem can be solved from the same level of consciousness that created it.'" It was all becoming clear.

William concluded, "So, if humans start designing stuff that follows the assumption that nature knows what it's doing, where waste is no longer a thing, where we live *with* our environment and not just in it or on it, then we'll be following a natural growth model."

Indeed, standing at that memorial reminded me of my life's journey. I once read that enlightenment occurs when an individual transcends desire and suffering to attain nirvana. And for the first time, I believed that love conquers all. Love and humanity are necessities, not luxuries. Without them, humanity cannot survive. Bliss, I discovered, is found when we realize we are all connected. It exists in that space of unity. I was filled with love. For humanity, for history, for myself.

And so I married my sweetheart, my love, Britta.

I had come full circle. I remembered my attempt to plant a tree that would not have room for its roots to grow, the look on my nephew's face when he saw my frustration, and I bought him a bonsai tree instead. I was invited back to the United Nations to participate in the International Day of Peace, and I heard Desmond Tutu speak.

"Sisters and brothers," he preached, "we can survive only together. We can be human only together. We can be safe only together. We can be prosperous only together, together, together, together."

Years ago, I woke up, traumatized by violence. The answer that came to me then was to plant trees—to literally get back to the roots of nature and peace. But what I didn't understand then was that *I am the tree*. We are all the trees. We need to replant our roots and rejoin the global interconnected system of life. By becoming one with the world, we become one with each other. And then we will all be rooted in peace.

To Write to the Author

If you wish to contact the author or would like more information about this book, please write to the author in care of Llewellyn Worldwide, and we will forward your request. Both the author and publisher appreciate hearing from you and learning of your enjoyment of this book and how it has helped you. Llewellyn Worldwide cannot guarantee that every letter written to the author can be answered, but all will be forwarded. Please write to:

Greg Reitman
℅ Llewellyn Worldwide
2143 Wooddale Drive
Woodbury, MN 55125.2989

Please enclose a self-addressed stamped envelope for reply,
or $1.00 to cover costs. If outside the US, enclose
an international postal reply coupon.